SPEED CHESS CHALLENGE

KASPAROV

v

SHORT

1987

Nigel Short about to play a move while Gary Kasparov ponders.

SPEED CHESS CHALLENGE

KASPAROV

v

SHORT

1987

Raymond Keene

B. T. Batsford Ltd, *London*

in association with
Thames Television and Channel Four

A CHANNEL FOUR BOOK

First Published 1987

© Raymond Keene 1987

ISBN 0 7134 5784 8

Typeset by Turners Typesetting,
Halifax, West Yorkshire and
Printed in Great Britain by
Anchor Brendon Ltd., Tiptree, Essex
for the publishers, B. T. Batsford Ltd.,
4 Fitzhardinge Street, London W1H 0AH
in conjunction with Thames Television
and Channel 4 Television.

A BATSFORD CHESS BOOK
Adviser: R. D. Keene, GM, OBE
Technical Editor: P. A. Lamford

Contents

How to Use this Book

Notation

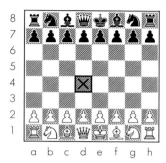

Figurine algebraic notation has now become universally accepted in chess publications. It is easy to learn and can be followed by chess players in all countries. The diagram above shows the starting position and how the squares are indicated.

The squares are represented, as in the game of battleships, by a letter followed by a number. Thus in the above diagram the white king is on e1, the black king on e8. If White advances his pawn on d2 by two squares, to the square marked with an ⊠, the move is shown as d4. If a piece (other than a pawn) moves to a square then the symbol for that piece is followed by the 'name' of the square, e.g. ♘f3. If it is possible for two pieces to move to the same square, the file or rank of departure is identified.

The Format of this Book

A special format has been used in this book to help readers who are relatively inexperienced in chess notation, or who wish to follow the games without using a chessboard. The format is based closely on that used in Batsford's pioneering work on the famous 1972 Fischer-Spassky World Title clash: *Fischer-Spassky, Move by Move* (Ken Smith and Larry Evans). After each white move _and_ each black move there is a diagram. The move just played is indicated clearly on the diagram by a square around that piece.

We sincerely hope that this format will help in your appreciation of the thrilling games which follow.

Rates of Exchange

For young or inexperienced players, or those taking an interest in chess again after a break, it is worth noting the respective values of the chess pieces. Assuming the basic currency unit of a pawn being equal to one point, the following values can be established:

PIECE	SYMBOL	VALUE
PAWN	♙	1
KNIGHT	♘	3
BISHOP	♗	3
ROOK	♖	5
QUEEN	♕	9
KING	♔	Priceless

In the endgame, when the king can emerge from its fortress to take an active part in the game, he has about the same value as a bishop or a knight. But if the king is checkmated, the game ends. It is, therefore, possible to sacrifice almost all of your pieces in order to deliver checkmate, so no true value can be placed on the king.

Explanation of Symbols Used in the Notes

+	Check
×	Captures/Takes
!	Excellent Move
!!	Brilliant Move
?	Weak Move
??	Blunder
!?	Interesting Move
?!	Dubious Move
0-0	Castles kingside
0-0-0	Castles queenside
. . .	indicates that a black move follows.
ep	*en passant*

The *en passant* capture is a special case when the opponent's pawn has moved two squares and you have a pawn on an adjacent file on your fifth rank. At the first opportunity <u>only</u>, you may capture that pawn as though it had moved only one square. An example appears on page 77 after Black's 16 . . . f5.

Acknowledgements

Many thanks to my wife, Annette, for valuable suggestions and for her speedy typing of this book; to Richard Sams for preparing the diagrams in manuscript and Turners Typesetting for producing quick and accurate proofs; to Paul Lamford and Peter Kemmis-Betty of B. T. Batsford; to Michael Feldman, the producer of the Thames Television series for Channel 4; to Thames Television Press Office for outstanding photographs; to Andrew Page for helping to stage the match and the London Docklands Development Corporation for their sponsorship support. Also to Peter Stringfellow of Stringfellows and The Hippodrome for his hospitality.

Ray Keene, London, March 1987

Bibliography

Weltgeschichte des Schachs 7: Steinitz (David Hooper / Wildhagen)

The Centenary Match, Kasparov-Karpov III (Keene and Goodman / B. T. Batsford)

Batsford Chess Openings (Kasparov and Keene / B. T. Batsford)

The Oxford Companion to Chess (Hooper and Whyld / Oxford University Press)

Fischer-Spassky 1972 Move by Move (Smith and Evans / B. T. Batsford)

"What do you mean I've got the wrong-coloured dinner jacket?"

The magnificent stage at London's Hippodrome while play was being filmed by Thames Television for Channel 4.

Why the Speed Chess Challenge?

With the staging of the first half of the 1986 Centenary World Chess Championship in London, the British capital has become a major world centre for chess. Many of those involved with that triumph believed that the initiative had to be pursued.

The Speed Chess Challenge was conceived jointly by David Elstein and Michael Feldman of Thames Television. It was made possible by the generous sponsorship of the London Docklands Development Corporation, who have sponsored many important chess events in London since 1984.

The concept was to bring together two of the greatest, most dangerous and innovative Grandmasters in the world. One, World Champion, Gary Kasparov, is, perhaps, the most exciting and dynamic world champion in the entire hundred years since the supreme chess title was introduced. The other, Nigel Short, is Britain's leading player, an intuitive genius and the most likely western threat to Kasparov's crown.

The match format was to be in keeping with the forceful, modern image of the players: six games, played over two days (4 and 5 February) at the fashionable London Hippodrome, equipped with back-up electronic display, music and laser show. For every game each player would have 25 minutes to complete all his moves. If the moves were not carried out within that space, time forfeiture and loss of the game would immediately result.

The event was specifically designed to attract a potentially vast TV audience who could be convinced of the fascination chess can hold. Great attention was paid to the décor and presentation. The players were dressed in elegant dinner jackets, white or black according to their colour in each game. Experienced presenter Tony Bastable, doyen of the Thames Television World Championship coverage, injected a human touch, introducing the players before each game and interviewing them afterwards as they had to face victory or defeat. I provided in-game commentary for viewers, while Dr John Nunn explained moves to the invited audience at the close of play. Arbiters in evening dress policing the play were: Lothar Schmid of West Germany, Louise McDonald of Australia and Bob Wade, OBE, of England, a truly international and expert team.

The invited audience were reminded by ticket, programme and regular pre-game announcements that 'In accepting our invitation to be present at these recordings, you are reminded that it is a condition that the moves and results are not made public prior to each game's transmission'.

The Thames Television sport production team were Executive Producer, Keith Mosedale; Producer, Michael Feldman; Director, Lewis Williams and Production Assistant, Carole Jeayes.

The London Docklands Development Corporation team were Eric Hollington-Pickering, Robert Clarke and Eddie Oliver.

Games were relayed to the spectators via state of the art computer technology using a giant video screen specially created and designed for Thames Television by Intelligent Chess Software's electronic wizards, David Levy and Kevin O'Connell.

There was general agreement amongst highly delighted spectators, experts and chess sponsors that this new and challenging format represents the best way forward for chess on television to rival bowls, darts and even the extremely successful game of snooker!

Profile of the World Champion, Gary Kasparov (USSR)

Gary Kasparov (born 13-4-63 in Azerbaijan in the Soviet Union) is World Chess Champion. His rating as of January 1987 is 2735, second only to Bobby Fischer's legendary 2780. At only 23, he is considered by many to be the most exciting and innovative player of all time.

Kasparov's rise to World Champion has been meteoric. He qualified as a Grandmaster in 1980 at the age of 17 and two years later he was rated as the second strongest player in the world. In November 1985, aged 22, he became the youngest world champion in the history of the official world championship. In recognition of his achievements Gary was honoured with the "chess oscar" in 1982, 1983, 1985 and 1986.

Kasparov first played a match in London in 1983, when he defeated Viktor Korchnoi in the Candidates' semi-final. This set him on the path to the World Championship.

During 1984 and 1985 Gary twice played Karpov for the world title, a total of 72 games. Then in the summer of 1986 he returned to London for the first half of the revenge world championship match (the second half being held in Leningrad) which he again won in convincing style. Kasparov has come to speak of Karpov in these mammoth matches as "my permanent opponent".

Gary has also found time to play a series of matches against top Grandmasters: Robert Hübner, Ulf Andersson, Jan Timman and Tony Miles (England's board one Olympiad team member) where his opponents suffered crushing defeats. Tony Miles ½ Kasparov 5½, for example.

Finally in December 1986 Kasparov won the very strong category 16 OHRA tournament in Brussels. During that event Gary lost his first game to Nigel, but won the second.

Kasparov-Short
OHRA **Brussels 1986**
Queen's Gambit Declined

1 d4 e6 2 ♘f3 ♘f6 3 c4 d5 4 ♘c3 ♗e7 5 ♗g5 h6 6 ♗×f6 ♗×f6 7 e3 0-0 8 ♖c1 c6 9 ♗d3 ♘d7 10 0-0 d×c4 11 ♗×c4 e5 12 h3 e×d4 13 e×d4 ♘b6 14 ♗b3 ♗f5 15 ♖e1 ♗g5 16 ♖a1 ♘d7 17 d5 ♖c8 18 ♘d4 ♗g6 19 ♘e6 f×e6 20 d×e6 ♔h7 21 ♕×d7 ♕b6 22 e7 ♖fe8 23 ♕g4 ♕c5 24 ♘e4 ♕×e7 25 ♗c2! ♖f8 26 g3 ♕d8 27 ♖ad1 ♕a5 28 h4 ♗e7

29 ♘c3! ♗×c2 30 ♖×e7 ♖g8 31 ♖dd7 ♗f5 32 ♖×g7+ ♔h8 33 ♕d4 Black resigns.

World Champion, Gary Kasparov.

Profile of Nigel Short, England's Top-Rated Grandmaster

Nigel Short (born 1-6-65 in Atherton in the North of England) is Britain's youngest, highest rated and most exciting Grandmaster (rated 2615 as of January 1987 — 7th in the world). Nigel is reigning British Quickplay Champion, having won the title last year with the maximum score of 11/11. Many experts consider him to be the main western contender for the world title.

Nigel was a child prodigy. At the age of six in 1971 he was taught the game by his father. In 1977, just three months before his 12th birthday, he qualified for the British Championship. He was the youngest to do so by four years. During that championship, the 12-year-old won a sensational game against 10-times British Champion, Dr Jonathan Penrose.

He became the youngest holder of the international master title in 1980. The previous year he had tied for first place in the British Championship, but lost on a tie-break to Robert Bellin. In 1980 he also took second place to Gary Kasparov in the junior world championships in Dortmund. Short won the BBC Television Master Game tournament in 1980 ahead of many seasoned Grandmasters. He won the British Championship outright for the first time in 1984 and qualified as a Grandmaster, at that time the youngest in the world.

Nigel was a member of the English Olympiad team which won the silver medals behind the USSR in Thessaloniki in 1984 and also in Dubai in 1986, where he won an individual gold medal.

In 1985 he became the first English player to qualify for the World Championship Candidates' tournament by winning the Interzonal play-off in Biel. Unfortunately, he did not come in the first four and will have to wait for the next cycle to be able to confront Gary Kasparov and perhaps wrest the world championship away from him.

Nigel raced to the lead in the powerful Wijk aan Zee tournament in January 1987 and went on to share first prize with Korchnoi (whom he beat in their individual game) in this great Dutch event.

Short-Kasparov
OHRA **Brussels 1986**
Sicilian Defence

1 e4 c5 2 ♘f3 d6 3 d4 c×d4 4 ♘×d4 ♘f6 5 ♘c3 a6 6 ♗e3 e6 7 ♕d2 b5 8 f3 ♘b8-d7 9 g4 h6 10 0-0-0 ♗b7 11 ♗d3 ♘e5 12 ♖he1 ♖c8 13 ♔b1 ♗e7 14 h4 b4 15 ♘a4 ♕a5 16 b3 ♘fd7 17 g5 g6 18 f4 ♘×d3 19 c×d3 h×g5 20 h×g5 d5 21 f5 e5 22 e×d5 ♕×d5 23 f6 ♗d6 24 ♘c2 a5 25 ♗a7 ♔f8 26 ♘e3 ♕e6 27 ♘c4 ♔g8 28 ♘×d6 ♕×d6 29 ♘b2 ♖c3 30 ♘c4 ♕d5 31 ♘e3 ♕e6 32 ♖c1 ♕a6 33 ♖×c3 b×c3 34 ♕×c3 ♕×a7 35 ♕c7 ♕d4 36 ♕×b7 ♕×d3+ 37 ♘c2 ♖h2 38 ♕c8+ ♘f8?

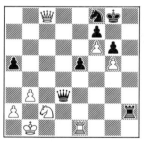

39 ♖×e5 ♖h1+ 40 ♔b2 ♕d2 41 ♖e8 ♕d6 42 ♖d8 ♕c5+ 43 ♔a3 ♔h7 44 ♖×f8 ♕d6+ 45 b4 Black resigns.

England's Number One, Nigel Short.

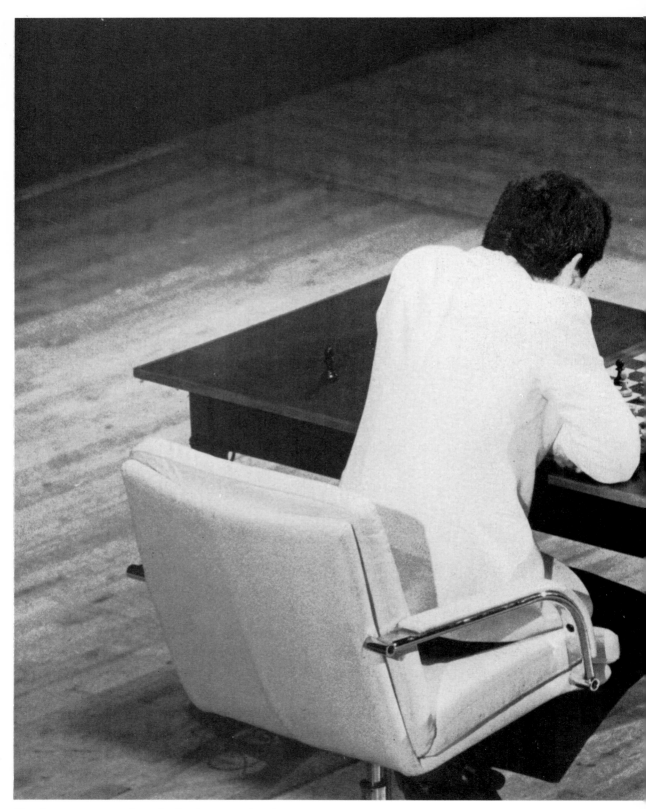

Total concentration from both players — the chairs seem too comfortable!

GAME ONE

White: Gary Kasparov   Black: Nigel Short
Dutch Defence

The specially invited audience at Peter Stringfellow's London Hippodrome was treated to a dramatic opening game. Short, playing the Dutch Defence, established an early initiative. This was surprising, since he was playing Black and taking Black against Kasparov is rather like facing the serve from Boris Becker.

In the middlegame, Gary recovered and won a pawn by means of some superfine tactics. However, the champion snatched one pawn too many and was exposed to a vicious counterattack from Nigel's rooks and knight.

With time running out and the moves coming in machine-gun-like bursts, Nigel lost that knight, but his position remained very threatening and he still missed chances to draw and notch up half a point.

In the final stages of the battle, Nigel sought to rush his army of pawns forwards on both flanks. Remember, if a pawn reaches your opponent's back rank it becomes a queen, and this is normally sufficient to win.

However, Kasparov had a dangerous pawn of his own and when this hurtled inexorably towards the queening square, Short resigned.

A sparkling start to the match.

1 d4

Kasparov's favourite move and the one with which he inflicted so much damage on the previous champion, Anatoly Karpov, in their two world title matches of 1985 and 1986.

1 . . . e6

A flexible reply inviting the French Defence after 2 e4, but Kasparov declines the invitation.

2 ♘f3   **f5**

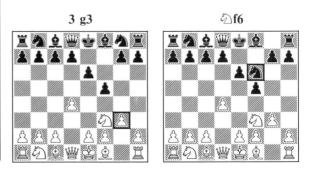

The Dutch Defence, usually an indication of aggressive intentions against the white king's wing. The World Champion reacts by fortifying his kingside in preparation for castling, developing his king's bishop in "fianchetto" on g2.

3 g3   **♘f6**

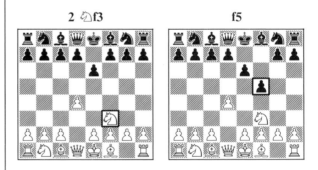

4 &g2

d5

7 b3

Preparing to play &a3, challenging the more active of Black's pair of bishops.

5 c4

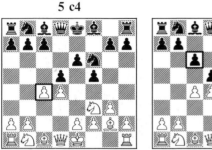

c6

7 ... ♕e7!

Of course Black does not pursue the chimera of gaining an extra pawn after 5 . . . d×c4? since 6 ♕a4+ c6 7 ♕×c4 would regain the material and leave Black's pawns broken up. With his 5th move Short establishes the so-called "Stonewall" variation of the Dutch Defence. It is, conventionally, regarded as strategically suspect. In particular, the black queen's bishop is hemmed in by pawns and could become permanently inactive. Nevertheless, Black's firm grip in the centre, especially his influence over the e4 square, grants him significant counterchances. Kasparov now resolves to castle his king into safety.

A fine move which, by reinforcing Black's bishop on d6, prevents White from executing his plan of &a3.

8 a4

6 0-0

&d6

Kasparov insists on playing &a3 and for this purpose he lends added protection to the key square (a3) from his rook on a1. Unfortunately, this move wastes time and weakens the square b4. In the game between the English Master, Glenn Flear (playing White) and Nigel Short (Black) from Nigel's great tournament triumph at Wijk aan Zee, Holland, the previous week, the identical position was reached. There Flear tried 8 ♘e5, when there ensued: 8 . . . 0-0 9 ♘d3 b6 10 &b2 ♘bd7 11 ♘d2 a5 12 ♖c1 with a balanced position.

"I have to be careful here; I'm sure he's got some trick up his sleeve."

8 . . . 0-0

9 ♗a3

All according to plan.

9 . . . ♗×a3

10 ♘×a3

Kasparov has achieved his aim of swapping the dark-squared bishops, but now his queeen's knight is placed somewhat clumsily on a3. Knights, being short-range pieces, are often poorly situated if they get stuck at the extreme edge of the board.

10 . . . ♘bd7

Black continues sensibly with the development of his forces, but he could have considered 10 . . . a5, fixing the weakness on b4.

11 a5

Kasparov promptly stops this idea by playing a5 himself, advancing into Black's terrain.

11 . . . b6

To challenge White's pawn on a5 and preparing to develop his bishop on b7.

12 ♕d2

An unexpected move, since the black knight can now attack the white queen, driving it away with gain of time. Nevertheless, this is not serious for White since the queen is heading for a superior post.

12 ... ♘e4

13 ♕b2　　　　**♗b7**

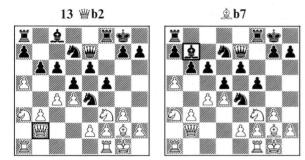

The players have now completed their development and they must each seek to establish a plan for the middlegame battle to come. Broadly speaking, development may be considered complete when a player's rooks are connected with each other, as is the case with both positions here.

14 b4?

But this ambitious advance is wrong and was severely criticised by Kasparov himself in discussions with Short after the game. White should play the cautious 14 ♘c2. This retreat of the white queen's knight would fulfil several functions:

　1) there would be a threat of a6 from White;
　2) the sensitive b4 square is defended;

3) the white knight relocates to bolster up the white centre.

Kasparov's choice in the game exposes him to a severe counterattack.

14 ... b×a5

15 b×a5　　　　**♖ab8**

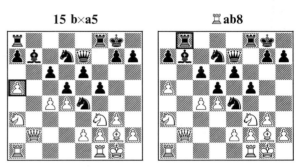

Kasparov's queen, his most powerful piece, is now uncomfortable, facing the black rook on the open b-file.

16 ♖fb1　　　　**c5**

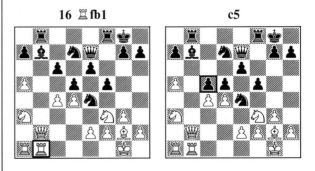

Black stirs up action in the centre of the board. Also excellent is Kasparov's suggestion of 16 ... ♗a6 opening fire against the white queen from the black rook and placing the black bishop on a more active square.

17 ♕c1

The white queen slips away from the annoying pressure created by the black rook.

17 . . . ♖fc8

Once again a black rook faces the white queen, and once again the white queen is forced to escape.

18 ♕e3   **c×d4**

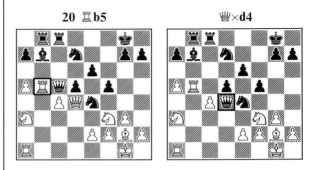

19 ♕×d4

Threatening ♕×a7.

19 . . . ♕c5

This move, played immediately by Short, forces the exchange of queens.

20 ♖b5   **♕×d4**

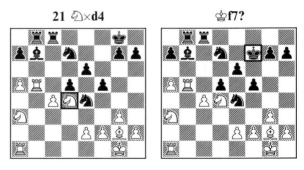

21 ♘×d4   **♔f7?**

Later, both players were to castigate this as an error. The simple 21 . . . d×c4 is fine for Black. Now Kasparov is given an opportunity for one of those bomb-bursts of tactical brilliance for which he is justly famous.

22 c×d5   **♗×d5**

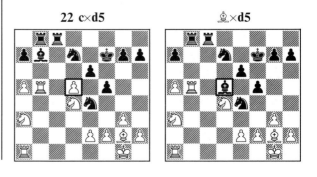

23 ♘×f5!!

What an unexpected coup. If Black replies 23 . . . e×f5 then 24 ♖×d5 or 23 . . . ♖×b5 24 ♘×b5 e×f5 25 ♗×e4 ♗×e4 26 ♘d6+ forking Black's king, rook and bishop. Kasparov took just seven seconds to spot all of this! Short, on the contrary, was visibly shocked and used up well over a minute of his precious thinking time to find a reply.

23 . . . ♘df6

24 ♗×e4   ♘×e4

A forced recapture, otherwise White continues with ♘d6+.

25 f3

Absolutely typical of Kasparov. Rather than retreat his own attacked knight, he threatens his opponent's.

25 . . . e×f5

26 ♖×d5   ♘c3

With a double attack against White's rook and pawn on e2. Best for White here is 27 ♖d2! defending the pawn and leaving White one pawn ahead with good chances to win the game. But Kasparov, having collected one pawn, assumed that Short had accidentally lost another. The World Champion now proceeds to snatch the black pawn on f5 without appreciating the dangers involved.

27 ♖×f5+?   ♔e6

Suddenly White's rook is stranded and in trouble.

28 e4

The only way to protect e2 and f5.

28 . . . g6

Nudging the white rook again. This piece is now extremely pushed for a decent safety square.

29 ♖g5

Obligatory, for if 29 ♖f4? ♘e2+ forks White's king and rook.

29 . . . ♖b2!

A powerful invasion imprisoning White's king on

its own back rank. If possible, it is good in 95% of cases to plant a rook on an opponent's second rank in this way. After such a move Short should not lose this game.

30 ♔h1

At this stage both players had just over nine minutes left to complete all of their remaining moves.

30 . . . ♔f6

31 h4

If now 31 . . . h6 persecuting White's rook, then the unfortunate piece eludes its hunters with 32 e5+ ♔f7 33 ♖g4. Short correctly prefers to attack White's group of kingside pawns.

Lonely figures in a vast theatre oblivious to the audience.

31 . . . ⧎f2

32 ⧎c1

Pinning Black's knight to the rook on c8.

32 . . . ⧎d8!

A neat trick, breaking the pin. White cannot play 33 ⧎×c3?? on account of 33 . . . ⧎d1 checkmate. In this line one can observe the power exerted by the rook established on White's second rank (⧎f2).

33 ♘c4

At least now White's knight can enter the battle. On c4 the knight performs the vital task of preventing Black from doubling his rooks along White's

second rank by . . . ⧎(d8)-d2. If that concentration of force could be achieved Kasparov would be in danger of losing in spite of his two extra pawns.

33 . . . ♘e2

34 ⧎b1   **⧎×f3**

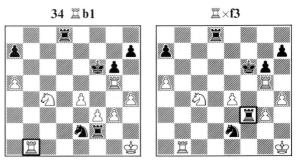

Regaining one pawn.

35 ♔g2

But White's king emerges from its dungeon.

35 . . . ⧎dd3

Piling up on the white pawn on g3. 36 g4? ♘f4+ is

clearly out of the question for White.

36 ♞e5

The white knight forks the two black rooks, but as yet there is no need to panic. Kasparov had 7 minutes left, Short 5½.

36 ... ♜×g3+

37 ♔f2!

The only move to retain chances of a win. If instead 37 ♜×g3 ♜×g3+ 38 ♔f2 ♔×e5 when Black has no problems at all.

37 ... ♜c3

Not 37 ... ♜×g5 38 ♞×d3 when Black's rook and knight are both under attack.

38 ♞g4+   ♔e6

Black is forced to sacrifice his knight, but the black rooks remain on the rampage and White's army is scattered, so Short still has excellent chances to hold the draw.

39 ♔×e2   ♜c2+

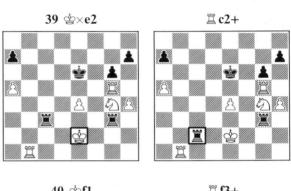

40 ♔f1   ♜f3+

41 ♔e1   ♜h3

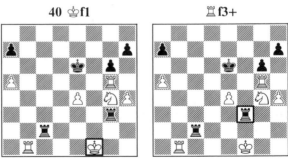

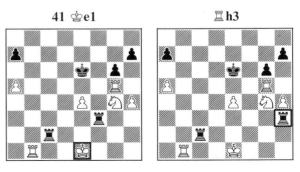

With horrible threats such as ... ♜×h4 or ...

♖h1 checkmate. Kasparov desperately tries to disentangle his pieces and regroup them for a counterattack against the black king.

42 ♖e5+

♔d6

43 ♖d1+

♔c6

44 ♘f2

The knight returns to prevent the deadly ... ♖h1.

44 ... ♖×h4?

With his time running out, Short commits the final, fatal error. Nigel had just over two minutes now for all of his moves, but if he had thought a little longer he would have found salvation in 44 ... ♖e3+! 45 ♔f1 ♖f3! which wins White's knight. Kasparov would then have been forced to play for a draw himself with 46 ♖e6+. Having lost the thread in the time-scramble at this moment, Nigel is never given a second bite.

45 ♖d8

The threat is ♖c8+, skewering Black's king and rook on c2.

45 ... ♖a2

46 ♖ed5

Co-ordination has been achieved. Black is now in extreme danger from White's passed pawn on e4, which has a clear path to run to e8 where it would promote to a queen.

46 ... ♖h2

47 ♖d2

Sensibly sacrificing the irrelevant pawn on a5 in order to deflate the pressure exerted by the black rooks still acting in unison on White's second rank.

47 ... ♖×a5

48 ♖c2+   ♔b7

49 ♖d7+   ♔b6

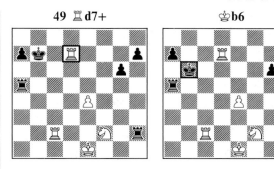

50 ♖d3

White's position is now perfectly safe and he will soon be ready to advance his central pawn. The only danger is Black's own pawn mass on g6 and h7, but this infantry batallion is too far back to cause White serious difficulties.

50 ... ♖b5

51 ♖d6+   ♔b7

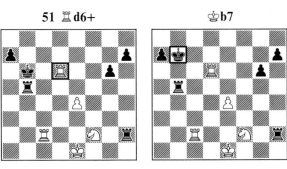

Kasparov had over 3½ minutes in hand, Nigel just 2, but the black position is lost and Kasparov only needed a few seconds of rapid-fire play to finish him off.

52 ♔f1   **g5**

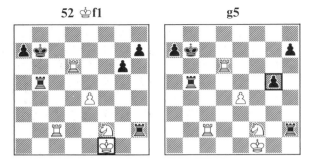

The advance is too slow.

53 ♔g1   **♖h4**

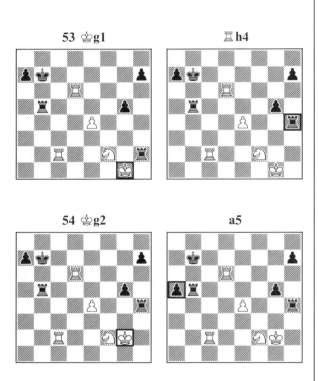

54 ♔g2   **a5**

Nigel tries his luck on the other wing, but there is no way that he will be in time.

55 ♘d3!

Inviting the trap 55 . . . ♖×e4? 56 ♘c5+, forking

Black's king and rook. In endgames of this sort the knight, because of its double-attack ability, can be a really tricky piece.

55 . . . ♖g4+

56 ♔f3   **♖g1**

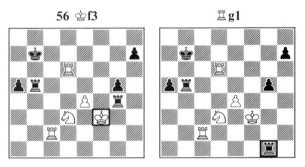

57 e5

From d3 the white knight also covers the Coronation March of this pawn.

57 . . . g4+

58 ♔f2

♖gb1

60 ♔g2

h5

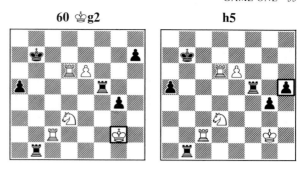

59 e6

This pawn will cost Black at least a rook.

59 ... ♖f5+

61 e7

Black resigns

The white e-pawn cannot be prevented from becoming a queen when it reaches e8. Black could only avoid this by making ruinous material sacrifices. At the end of play Kasparov had three minutes left, Short one.

SCORE SO FAR:

	1	2	3	4	5	6
Kasparov	1					
Short	0					

GAME TWO

White: Nigel Short Black: Gary Kasparov
Sicilian Defence

Nigel's first White in the match and he seemed determined to strive for a win. His opening play was extremely aggressive, storming forwards with his massed pawns on the king's flank.

The World Champion hates defensive play and launched a second front, sacrificing a pawn to tangle up White's pieces and create open files and diagonals for his own forces. Many experts doubted the soundness of this sacrifice, but in the heat of the battle it was extremely difficult to refute Kasparov's ingenious idea.

In a fearfully complex situation Nigel could have held on, but, in trying to grab a stray black rook, he overlooked a cunning switchback manœuvre by Kasparov's queen and dark-squared bishop. After that, Nigel's position became a smoking ruin, full of weak points.

Kasparov wrapped up neatly in the rook and pawn endgame, picking off White's remaining pawns like over-ripe fruit.

1 e4

Nigel's preferred opening move, which usually leads to more volatile, fluid positions than Kasparov's favourite, 1 d4.

1 . . . c5

The Sicilian Defence, Black's most aggressive and ambitious counter to 1 e4. Legend has it that this defence acquired its name from the analysis of the Sicilian Priest, Pietro Carrera. In 1617 he produced his book *Il Gioco degli Scacchi* (*The Game of Chess*) which not only contained his work on the Defence 1 e4 c5, but also some alarming advice for the prospective match player:

> "He must abstain some days from meat to clear his brain as also to let blood, he should take both purgatives and emetics to drive the humours from his body, and he must above all be sure to confess his sins and receive spiritual absolution just before sitting down to play in order to counteract the demoniacal influence of magic spells."

2 ♘f3

Preparing to enter the standard anti-Sicilian variation.

2 . . . d6

Main alternatives here are: 2 . . . e6, 2 . . . ♘c6, 2 . . . ♘f6 and sometimes 2 . . . g6.

3 d4   **c×d4**

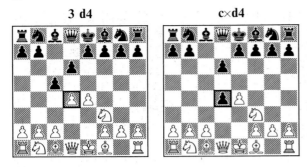

Black must challenge the formation of White's broad pawn centre.

4 ♘×d4   **♘f6**

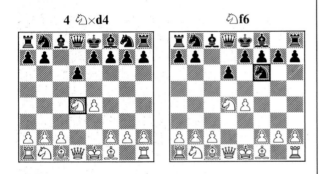

5 ♘c3   **a6**

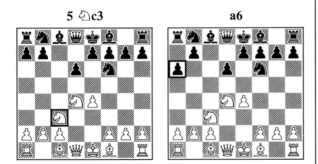

The position before us is one of the most fashionable lines in the popular Sicilian. It is known as the Najdorf Variation after the famous Polish/Argentine Grandmaster, Miguel Najdorf. Black runs the risk of delaying his development, and is often overrun by a swift White offensive right in the opening stage. However, in compensation, Black's position is solid and flexible. He already possesses a useful majority of pawns in the centre of the board and he has the possibility of expanding to gain territory on the queen's wing with . . . b5.

6 ♗e3

Short's favourite, though highly regarded alternatives are available, such as 6 ♗e2 (Anatoly Karpov's choice); 6 ♗g5 (often used by John Nunn); 6 f4; 6 ♗c4 and 6 h3 (both practised by Bobby Fischer) and even 6 a4.

6 . . . e6

In theory, Black's small cluster of central pawns on d6 and e6 should now be bomb-proof, but so often in practice White succeeds in landing some devastating sacrificial blow before Black has fully mobilised his forces. This is what happened at Brussels in December when Short beat Kasparov for the first time (see page 14). Then Short chose 7 ♕d2; now he varies, perhaps fearing an improvement cooked up by Kasparov's home analysis.

7 f3

Defending his pawn on e4 and providing a firm basis for a vigorous onslaught by his kingside pawns.

"How do I get through to his king?"

7 ... ♘bd7

8 g4

A remarkably aggressive display by Nigel. But, of course, the onrush of the white pawns leaves certain weak and exposed points in their wake, should Black be able to counterattack.

8 ... h6

To stop 9 g5.

9 h4

Consistent aggression.

9 ... b5

Kasparov strikes his claim to territory on the other wing. The immediate intention, if he is given time, will be to continue with . . . ♗b7.

10 ♖g1

Threatening g5 in earnest. Naturally 10 g5 is harmless after 10 . . . h×g5 when 11 h×g5?? loses to . . . ♖×h1.

10 ... g6!

Prophylaxis. Kasparov cleverly prevents White from ravaging his kingside with g5 followed by an advance of the white g-pawn to g6.

11 g5   **h×g5**

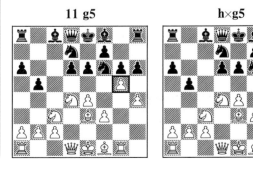

12 h×g5   **♘h5**

14 ♘c6   **♕c7**

A further point of 10 . . . g6 was to anchor a firm base on h5 for Black's king's knight.

15 ♘×b4

13 a4

White has duly collected the pawn, but his knight has been diverted to a weird square. If Black were now to play the natural 15 . . . d5, opening fire on the clumsy knight with the black bishop from f8, then White could restore cohesion to his army by sacrificing a piece, viz: 16 ♘b×d5 e×d5 17 ♘×d5 with excellent compensation for his material investment of knight against three pawns. But Kasparov has a totally different scheme in mind.

Very ambitious indeed. The sudden attack on b5 seems to force 13 . . . b×a4, when Black's whole queenside pawn constellation is broken up. Nevertheless, the ever alert Kasparov finds an ingenious counter. The orthodox move for Short at move 13 would have been 13 ♕d2 to be followed by 0-0-0.

15 . . . ♗g7!

With his pawn sacrifice Kasparov has totally changed the nature of the position. Instead of White being on the offensive, he now has an extra pawn, but is forced to defend. The black bishop is operating along an extremely dangerous diagonal from g7, the black queen is active on the c-file from c7, and soon the black queen's rook will set up enormous pressure on the b-file from b8. The situation has become difficult for Short to handle psychologically, and especially so in practical play at a speed chess time limit.

13 . . . b4!?

A fascinating idea. Kasparov sacrifices a pawn to deflect White from his own attacking plans. After the game Grandmasters at the Hippodrome argued for hours as to whether this bold idea could possibly be correct.

16 ♘d3

Short offers to return the pawn at once. Indeed, any other course would involve him in insuperable pitfalls, e.g. 16 ♕d2 ♖b8! 17 ♘d3 ♖xb2! 18 ♘xb2 ♗xc3, winning White's queen.

16 ... ♖b8!

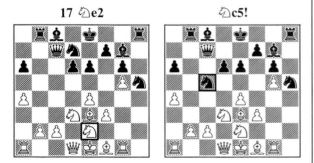

Kasparov elects to screw up the pressure to greater levels, rather than recoup his material by means of 16 ... ♗xc3+ 17 bxc3 ♕xc3+ 18 ♔f2, when most of White's problems would be behind him. The threat is now 17 ... ♖xb2 18 ♘xb2 ♗xc3+, winning two pieces for a rook.

17 ♘e2   ♘c5!

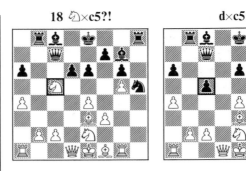

Not 17 ... ♗xb2? 18 ♘xb2 ♖xb2 19 ♗d4 forking Black's rooks. Kasparov's move challenges one of the lynchpins of White's defence, namely the knight on d3. After this move White should consider 18 ♘ec1!?

18 ♘xc5?!   dxc5

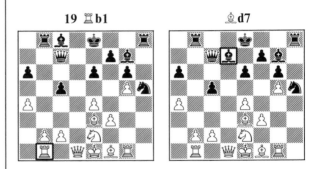

The exchange of knights has revealed a fresh diagonal for Black's queen from c7-h2. This could be a possible avenue for future invasion of the white position.

19 ♖b1   ♗d7

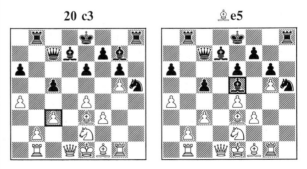

Attacking the a4 pawn. Of course Black does not fall for 19 ... ♖xb2? 20 ♖xb2 ♗xb2 21 c3! when the black bishop is cut off and in danger, e.g. to ♕b3.

20 c3   ♗e5

A powerful centralisation manœuvre which reinforces Black's pressure along the c7-h2 diagonal. It is important to prevent White from consolidating by playing f4. Normally, one is well advised to castle early in the game. Here, interestingly, White can no longer legally castle at all, while Kasparov avoids ... 0-0, in order to utilise to maximum effect his king's rook standing on the potentially open h-file.

21 ♖g4

A curious way of fighting for control of f4. 21 ♖h1 looks more natural, opposing Black's rook and knight down the h-file.

21 . . . ♘g3

Now there exists extreme danger of penetration from the black rook which may swoop into sensitive squares such as h1 or h2. For the moment, Nigel copes well with the invasion.

22 ♗g2   **♖h2**

This looks alarming, but White's resources are still adequate to stave off defeat.

23 ♔f2!

The king enters the battle as a valuable defensive piece.

23 . . . ♘×e2

24 ♕×e2   **♗×c3**

Regaining the pawn inasmuch as 25 b×c3 fails to 25 . . . ♖×b1. Short should now play cautiously with 25 ♕c2! when 25 . . . ♗e5 26 ♕×c5 ♕×c5 27 ♗×c5 ♖×b2+ 28 ♖×b2 ♗×b2 leads to a completely level ending, which would be drawn. Instead, Short spots a chance to pounce on Kasparov's stray rook on h2, but in so doing plunges headlong into a deadly and cunning trap.

25 ♗f4?

Seems to win either Black's queen or his rook by virtue of the double attack.

25 . . . ♗e5!!

Only now did Short realise the deep point of Kasparov's idea. If 26 ♗×h2 Black has the amazing switchback manoeuvre 26 . . . ♗d4+ 27 ♔e1 ♕×h2 with a winning attack, e.g. 28 ♗f1 ♗c3+ 29 ♔d1 (if 29 b×c3? ♖×b1+ wins) 29 . . . ♗×a4+ 30 ♔c1 ♕e5 and 31 b×c3 fails to . . . ♕×c3+. This fierce line, where the white king is hunted all along the back rank, was demonstrated by Kasparov himself immediately after the game.

White cannot defend his pawn on a4. If 28 a5? ♖×g5 29 f4 ♕d4+ and White collapses. He therefore makes the best of a desperate situation and stops . . . ♕d4+.

26 ♗×e5

There is no choice.

26 . . . ♕×e5

27 ♔g1

♖h5

28 ♕d2

28 . . . ♗×a4

29 f4

♕d4+

A pawn ahead, Kasparov has no objection to trading queens.

30 ♕×d4

c×d4

31 ♗f1

♗c2

Now White's weak pawns begin to fall off like rotten fruit in a storm.

32 ♖a1   **♗×e4**

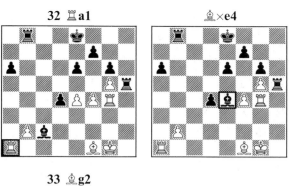

33 ♗g2

To prevent . . . ♖h1+.

33 . . . ♗×g2

34 ♖×g2   **♖h4**

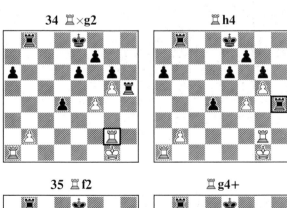

35 ♖f2   **♖g4+**

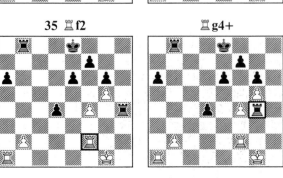

36 ♔h2   **e5!**

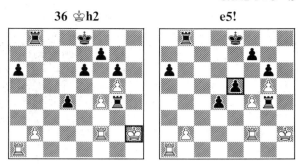

Completing the demolition of White's kingside pawns.

37 f×e5

An illusory grain of hope might have been offered by ♖e1, but then comes 37 . . . ♔d7! (threatening . . . ♖h8 mate) 38 ♔h3 ♖×f4 winning easily.

37 . . . ♔e7

Once again, the threat is . . . ♖h8 checkmate.

38 ♔h3   **♖×g5**

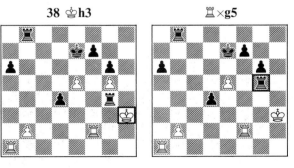

Renewing the threat.

39 ♔h4   **♖×e5**

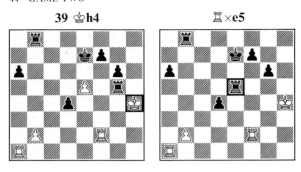

40 ♖×a6   **♖b7**

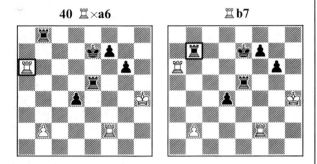

To stop ♖a7+. Black is now two pawns up and winning very easily.

41 ♖af6   **♔e8**

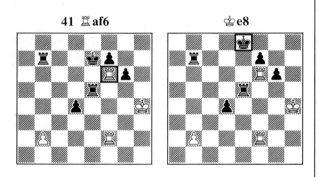

Accurate to the last. Not 41 ... ♔f8? 42 ♖×g6! exploiting the f-file pin.

42 ♖d6   **♖eb5**

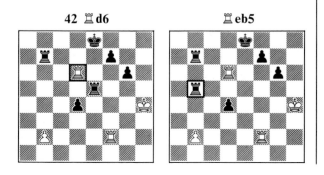

43 ♖e2+   **♔f8**

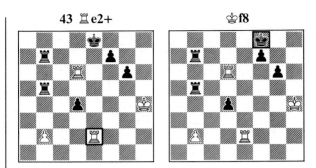

44 ♖×d4   **♖×b2**

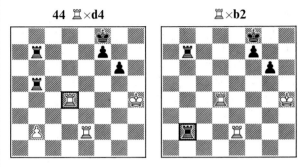

Eliminating White's final pawn. There is no fight left in the white position.

45 ♖d8+   **♔g7**

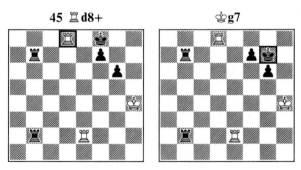

46 ♖ee8   **♖7b4+**

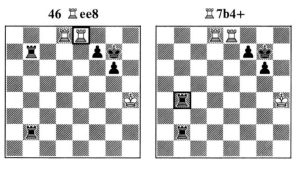

47 ♔g3

♖b4-b3+

48 ♔f4

♖f2+

49 ♔g4

f5+

50 ♔g5

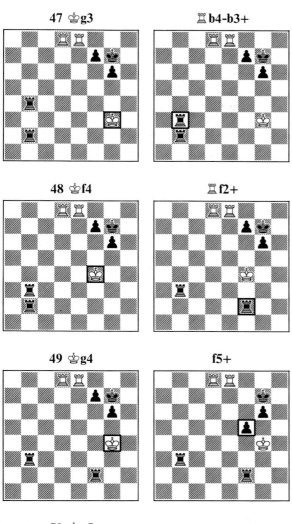

With the token threat of ♖d7 or ♖e7 mate.

50 . . . ♖g2+

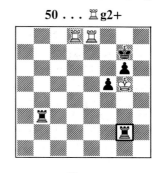

51 ♔f4

♖g4+

52 ♔e5

♖e4+

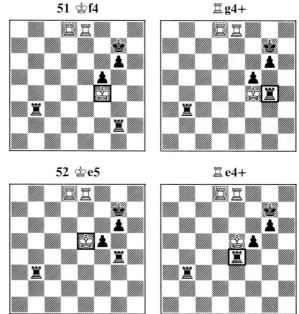

White resigns

The exchange of one pair of rooks is forced, after which Short would be two pawns down for nothing.

SCORE SO FAR:

	1	2	3	4	5	6
Kasparov	1	1				
Short	0	0				

GAME THREE

White: Gary Kasparov   Black: Nigel Short

Chigorin's Defence

Nigel scores his first win, and the VIP audience at The Hippodrome go wild with applause and cheering. The British Grandmaster had been so close to draws in both of the first two games and now he had landed a direct hit.

Nigel's defence with Black was unorthodox, obviously hoping to sidestep Kasparov's vast, encyclopædic knowledge of standard opening variations. Short appeared to be running serious risks, but the shock element worked to his advantage and the World Champion permitted a blocked, equal position to arise.

Nigel then offered a sacrifice of the exchange (rook for bishop) to obtain strategic compensation, in the form of domination over important central squares. Kasparov delayed acceptance of this sacrifice, but when he eventually decided to seize the material, the board burst into flames. White's forces broke into the black position on the queen's wing while Nigel whipped up a fierce counter-attack against the white king.

At this point the World Champion went astray. Instead of prudently withdrawing his pieces into consolidating defence around his own king, he poured his army right into the heart of the black fortress. Here, instead of delivering the hoped-for death blow, White's rooks and queen became cut off. Nigel briskly retaliated with an amazing pincer attack by both his king and his queen. With Black's king marching, incredibly, directly against his own, and faced with mighty threats from the invading black queen, the World Champion was forced to concede his first defeat.

1 ♘f3

A good, sound and solid developing move instead of Kasparov's habitual 1 d4.

1 . . . d5

Short occupies the centre with a pawn in classically approved fashion.

2 d4

Heading for a Queen's Gambit after 2 . . . ♘f6 3 c4. But Short has other, more adventurous ideas.

2 . . . ♗g4!?

Very unusual indeed. Further evidence, in fact that Short's opening play as Black in this match is expressly designed to throw the computer-brained Kasparov off the beaten track.

3 ♘e5

The knight leaps into the centre, attacking Black's bishop in the process. It is not easy to find precedents for this strange opening variation. One example is the game Steinitz–Chigorin, second World Championship game, Havana 1889. That had gone 3 ♘e5 ♗h5 4 ♕d3 ♕c8 5 c4 f6 6 ♘f3 e6 7 ♘c3 ♗g6 8 ♕d1 c6 9 e3 ♗d6 10 ♗d2 ♘e7. The strategic similarities with the opening of this Kasparov–Short game are evident. Wilhelm Steinitz (1836-1900) was the first official World Chess Champion, a title he gained in 1886 and held till 1894. Born in Prague, Steinitz was the founder of the modern 'strategic' style of chess. His opponent in that title match, Mikhail Ivanovich Chigorin (1850-1908) was the father of the Soviet School of Chess. The beautiful Leningrad Chess Club is now named in his honour.

3 ... ♗f5

4 c4

Attacking the black centre. From Kasparov one might have expected something wild and attacking such as 4 g4!? ♗e4 5 f3 ♗g6 6 h4.

4 ... f6

And here, knowing the World Champion's reputation for unbridled aggression, I had been anticipating 5 c×d5 f×e5 6 d×e5, with two centre pawns for the piece, but after 6 ... e6! this adventure cannot be regarded as sound.

5 ♘f3

Offering a gambit pawn which Black dare not accept, e.g. 5 ... d×c4? 6 ♘c3! with the threat of e4 to be followed by ♗×c4. Kasparov leaves this gambit on for some time to come.

5 ... c6

Short prefers to reinforce his central pawn on d5.

6 ♘c3

e6

"This is worrying — he's attacking me with the black pieces."

Once again, if 6 . . . d×c4 7 e4! ♗e6 (hoping to cling to the pawn on c4) 8 d5 c×d5 9 e×d5 to be followed by ♗×c4. In this variation White's lead in mobilisation would be decisive. This line is an excellent illustration of how dangerous it can be to go hunting pawns in the opening while neglecting development of the pieces. Short naturally avoids such pitfalls and continues constructing a Maginot line in the centre of the board.

9 . . . 0-0

7 g3

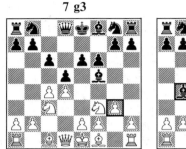

♗b4

8 ♗g2

♘e7

9 0-0

Even now Short does not dare abandon his central bastions and capture the loose pawn on c4, though White's compensation after 9 . . . d×c4 10 e4 ♗g4 is less clear than in the previous gambit variations.

10 ♕b3

At last Kasparov defends his pawn on c4 and in so doing attacks the black bishop on b4.

10 . . . a5

Gaining space on the queenside and preparing a later . . . a4, attacking the queen.

11 a3

♗×c3

12 b×c3

14 ♕a2

♗g6

Kasparov rightly avoids 12 ♕×b7? ♘d7 13 b×c3 ♖b8 when his queen is in trouble. An old chess proverb, which is usually accurate, states that it is much too risky to capture your opponent's queen's knight's pawn (b-pawn) with your own queen. Many games have been lost in this fashion.

15 e4

White seizes the centre with a huge mass of pawns, extending from c3 to e4. The pressure against Black's pawn on d5 is intense, with a bombardment building up from White's queen on a2, bishop on g2 and pawns on c4 and e4. In view of this looming mid-board crisis, Short regroups his bishop into a defensive posture.

12 . . . ♘d7

Once again offering the pawn sacrifice which White cannot accept.

13 ♘d2

The knight drops back, preparing for the central thrust e4.

15 . . . ♗f7

Black's fortress is hard to breach, e.g. 16 e×d5 e×d5 17 c×d5 ♗×d5 18 ♗×d5+ ♘×d5 and Black stands well.

13 . . . a4

Forcing the white queen to retreat.

16 ♖b1

♖b8

17 ♕c2   b5!

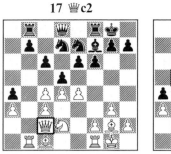

A powerful move. Short defends a4 and blocks the situation on the queen's wing where the World Champion was hoping to create some initiative. If White replies with 18 c5 then 18 . . . e5! leaves Black dictating the tempo of play in the centre.

18 c×d5   c×d5

Kasparov's choice has left him saddled with what is known as a weak, 'backward' pawn on c3, on the open c-file. This pawn forms a future target for the black rooks which can pile up against it on the c-file. The c3 pawn cannot be defended by another white pawn, so it is liable to become a serious focus for black pressure. What is worse, the square in front of it (c4) is totally under Black's control and could be occupied by a black piece, thus forming a pivot for a possible black attack.

19 ♕d3   ♕a5

20 ♖e1

White still succeeds in holding the balance, in spite of his weak pawn on c3, by generating counterplay down the e-file. White can aim at the slightly sensitive black pawn at e6 by ♗h3, and White retains the option of exchanging in the centre with e×d5 or pushing on with e5.

20 . . . ♖fc8

21 ♖b4

Physically shutting off the attack from Black's queen against the vulnerable c3 pawn.

21 . . . ♘c6

This forces the rook to withdraw, but, conversely, the black knight on c6 impedes the action of the rook operating from c8.

22 ♖b2

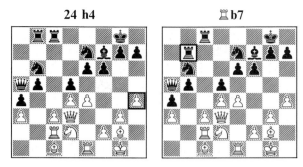

Dubious is 22 e×d5?! ♘×b4 23 c×b4 ♕b6 24 d×e6 ♗×e6 when White's compensation appears inadequate.

22 . . . ♘e7

23 ♖c2

Kasparov boldly strives for a win. If he were content with a draw the World Champion would have settled for the pusillanimous 23 ♖b4 ♘c6 with repetition of position.

23 . . . ♘b6

The black knight advances towards the strong outpost square on c4.

In order, at some stage, to double his rooks on the open c-file.

25 ♗h3

Threatening 26 e×d5, which Black promptly prevents by introducing lateral defence of his pawn on e6.

25 . . . ♖c6!

26 ♖b2

Offering the pawn on c3 in exchange for Black's pawn on b5. But Short refuses to co-operate.

26 . . . ♘c4!

If now 27 ♘×c4 b×c4 28 ♕c2 ♖b3! when Black's rook sunk in the white position gives him a clear advantage.

27 ♖b4   ♕c7

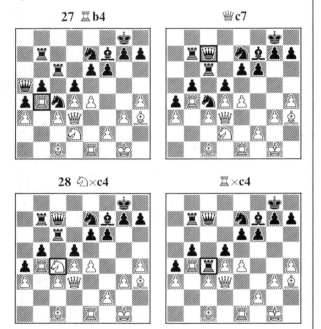

28 ♘×c4   ♖×c4

In this case 28 . . . b×c4 29 ♕b1 grants Black nothing since his rook cannot gain access to the key b3 square.

29 ♗d2

Of course, White does not fall for 29 ♖×c4? b×c4! Kasparov's move keeps the situation on the queenside under control. The bishop on d2 is a stalwart defender.

29 . . . ♕c6

30 e5   f5

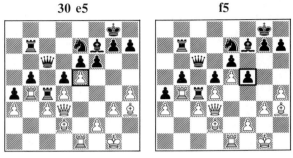

Short evidently does not wish the king's wing to be blasted open, so he blocks on this side too.

31 ♗f1

With a veiled threat against the black rook on c4.

31 . . . ♗h5

Black's bishop seizes an active diagonal.

"I thought there was something wrong with that move."

32 ♕e3   **h6!!**

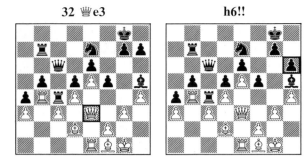

A brilliant move. First of all, Short stops White's intention of playing ♕g5, secondly he offers a profound sacrifice of his rook on c4 for White's light-squared bishop. If 33 ♗×c4 d×c4 followed by . . . ♘d5. Black would then dominate the whole board by means of his light-square control, while White would be condemned to utter passivity. Kasparov would never consent to such a humiliation, therefore he declines the sacrifice for the moment.

33 ♖eb1   **♔f7**

34 ♖1b2   **♔g8**

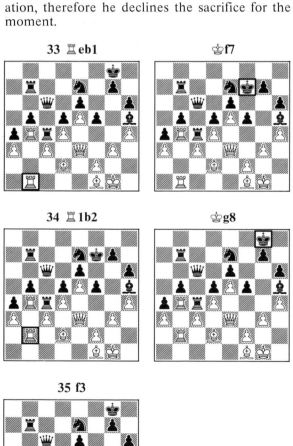

35 f3

Envisaging possible future aggression based on the plan ♗e2 and then g4.

35 . . . ♕a6

36 ♖b1   **♘c6**

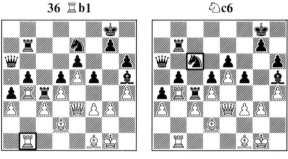

A crisis has been reached. Now that Black's knight has stirred from its post on e7 to attack White's rook at b4, Kasparov feels that he can at last accept the sacrifice.

37 ♗×c4   **d×c4**

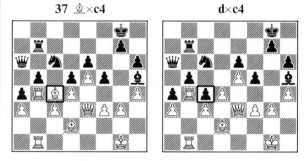

Not 37 . . . ♘×b4? 38 ♗×b5! followed by ♖×b4.

38 ♖4b2   **♘e7**

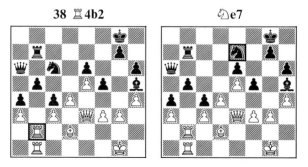

Planning . . . ♘d5, with absolute domination, as in my note to 32 . . . h6. But in the meantime

Kasparov has succeeded in deploying his rooks on the b-file. That fact gives him the opportunity for a tactical breakthrough which he immediately seizes.

39 d5!!

This is the type of move which inexperienced players find hard to visualise, but White must play it to gain breathing space for his queen and rooks. Otherwise . . . ♘d5 will throttle him.

39 . . . ♘×d5

40 ♕c5

Black cannot protect b5 against the combined onslaught of White's queen and two rooks. It looks as if Kasparov, having been tied up for so long, is about to unleash a victorious counterattack.

40 . . . ♗×f3

41 ♖×b5   **♖c7**

Of course, Black cannot afford to exchange rooks on b5 while he is material down.

42 ♖b8+   **♔h7**

43 ♕f8?

Having penetrated Black's line of defence with his heavy battalions, Kasparov wheels his troops sharp right to batter the enemy king. But this violent gesture turns out to be misguided. Correct is 43 ♕f2! ♗g4 44 ♖d8! In this case the queen guards the white king from possible threats, while White's own attack can proceed via ♖b1-b8.

43 . . . ♕a7+

An ominous check, the sign of things to come.

44 ♔f1

♖e7!!

White had been threatening ♕g8+ and ♕×e6+. This splendid move rules out that possibility and additionally locks the door on White's queen from scurrying back to the defence of her own king.

45 ♖1b2?

A better chance for a successful defence lay in 45 ♖e1!

There is a fantastic resource here, which Kasparov demonstrated to me after the game, namely 45 ♖1b7!? If now 45 . . . ♖×b7 46 ♕g8+ ♔g6 47 ♕×e6+ ♔h5 48 ♕×f5+ g5 49 ♕×f3+ wins for White. Better is 47 . . . ♘f6, when White can choose between 48 ♖×b7 ♕×b7 49 e×f6 or 48 e×f6!? ♖×b8 49 f7+ (discovered check from the white queen) 49 . . . ♔h7 50 ♕×f5+.

However, there is a considerably more energetic way to contest White's ingenious saving idea, namely 45 ♖1b7!? ♘e3+!! 46 ♗×e3 (if 46 ♔e1 ♖×b7 47 ♕g8+ ♔g6 48 ♕×e6+ ♔h5 and the difference is that the black knight on e3 defends f5) 46 . . . ♕×e3.

In this dramatic situation White is faced with the menace of . . . ♕e2+ and . . . ♕g2 mate. Therefore he must play 47 ♖b2! After 47 ♖b2! White threatens ♕×e7 while if Black moves his rook, e.g. 47 . . . ♖d7, then 48 ♕g8+ and ♕×e6+. The logical try is 47 . . . ♗g4 hoping for 48 ♕×e7 ♗h3+ 49 ♖g2 ♕f3+ regaining the rook and hounding the white king. After 47 . . . ♗g4 White can try 48 h5 ♗h3+ 49 ♖g2 but then comes 49 . . . ♕f3+ 50 ♔e1 and Black wins with 50 . . . ♕×c3+.

This must have been a colossally and unusually complicated position to analyse, especially in the few brief minutes left to the players at the close of this game.

45 . . . ♔g6!

A brilliant concept, rarely seen in grandmaster chess. With White's forces committed to an attack along the eighth rank, the black king advances out of danger and marches boldly forwards to attack its opposite number. Unless White stops this, the route chosen will be . . . ♔g6 . . . ♔h5 . . . ♔g4. With his clock time running out Kasparov must have been shattered by this highly unorthodox attack.

46 ♗c1

♔h5!!

The black king continues its singlehanded attack. In the commentary box I could scarcely believe the immense panache of Nigel's daring scheme.

47 ♖a8

In his confusion Kasparov actually drives the black queen into attack mode as well. White is soon crushed by simultaneous royal penetration on both flanks.

47 . . . ♕c5

49 . . . ♗×g4

48 ♖c8

♕×a3

50 ♖×c4

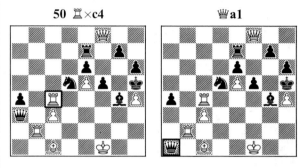

♕a1

49 g4+

White's moves show panic and desperation.

White resigns

There is no good way to protect the bishop on c1.

SCORE SO FAR:

	1	2	3	4	5	6
Kasparov	1	1	0			
Short	0	0	1			

GAME FOUR

White: Nigel Short   Black: Gary Kasparov
Sicilian Defence

The invited spectators at the Hippodrome were treated to a superb display of craftsmanship by the World Champion, who was evidently determined to avenge his defeat of the previous round.

Short's opening as White was restrained. He was content to exchange pieces and maintain the balance, leaving Kasparov the task of beating his head against a granite wall. This the Champion proceeded to do. He advanced a pawn on the queen's flank to a potentially menacing post; then he aquiesced in a mass exchange of rooks and queens. Finally, Gary brought his king into action, choosing the same path that Nigel had beaten with his own king in Game Three.

As the black king advanced, Nigel could have barred its track, but neglected to do so. A full-scale invasion promptly took place and as Nigel's time ran out the champion rained tactical blow after tactical blow on the tottering white position.

At the end, Nigel could not prevent a black pawn from pushing on to queen, so he resigned. Kasparov now had three points and could not lose the match, though if Nigel were to win both Games Five and Six he could still tie the overall score.

1 e4

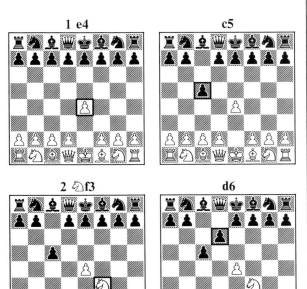

c5

2 ♘f3

d6

3 ♗b5+

Short varies from Game Two, where he played 3 d4. This bishop check is less common and not likely to cause Black severe problems in the opening.

3 . . . ♗d7

4 ♗×d7+

♕×d7

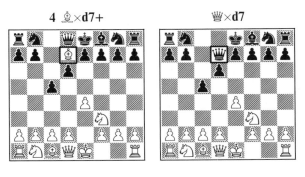

The trade of pieces has already relieved Black of many of his opening difficulties. White now has fewer pieces with which to inaugurate an attack.

5 0-0

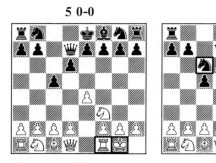

♘c6

6 c3

White intends to construct a powerful pawn centre by means of d4. Kasparov, of course, must take appropriate measures to avoid being crushed by an avalanche of white pawns in the middle of the board.

6 . . . ♘f6

7 ♕e2

White must protect his pawn.

7 . . . e6

8 d4

c×d4

9 c×d4

d5!

The correct antidote, a blockade erected on the light squares. White's next move is forced since 10 e×d5 ♘×d5 leaves White's pawn at d4 isolated and weak.

10 e5

White gains territory with this move and also attacks the black knight. However, there is some long-term strategic risk involved for White in that his pawn formation is gradually being fixed on dark squares. Since White's remaining bishop also operates on dark squares the mobility of this piece

"He's a tougher customer than I thought."

could become severely restricted by the obstacle of White's own pawns. In other words, White is in danger of getting a so-called 'bad bishop'.

10 ... ♘e4

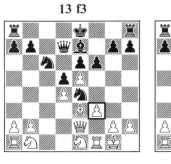

11 ♗e3

♗e7

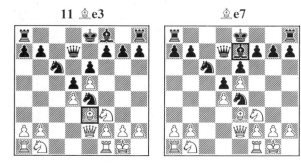

12 ♘e1

A curious-looking retreat, the point of which is to expel the black knight from its proud post on e4.

12 ... f6

Probing White's centre and also preparing an escape route for the knight on e4.

13 f3

♘g5

14 ♘d3

If 14 h4 Black's far-sighted 12th move provides a haven for the hunted knight on f7.

14 ... 0-0

15 ♘d2

♘f7

16 f4

White's trio of central pawns on d4, e5 and f4 is now totally secure. However, as I warned before, they are all pinned down on dark squares and thus represent an obstruction to White's bishop.

16 . . . b6

In order to cover the c5 square against a future ♘c5 by White.

17 ♘f3   **f5**

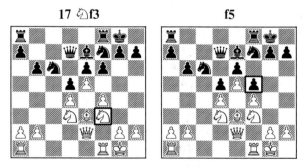

Kasparov seals up the kingside in preparation for the transference of the struggle to the opposite side of the board.

18 ♖ac1   **♖fc8**

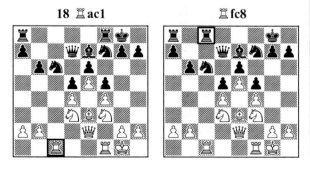

Since there is only one open file (the c-file) it is only natural that both players will mass their major pieces (rooks and queens) in this sector. It is likewise natural that all of these major pieces will be exchanged along this file. At the moment the position is approximately level and the game should be drawn. In fact, Short's next few moves indicate a waiting policy while Kasparov tries to stir up some action on the extreme left hand side of the board.

19 ♖c2   **♖c7**

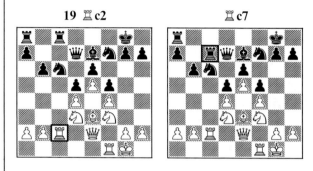

20 ♖fc1   **♖ac8**

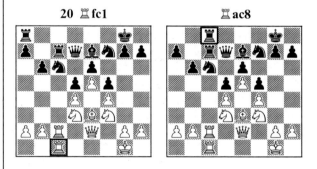

21 ♗d2   **h6**

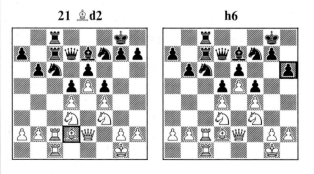

A long-range preparation for the aggressive advance . . . g5. Nevertheless, it is obviously too risky to try this in the middlegame while queens are still on the board.

22 h3   **a5**

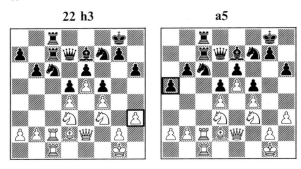

23 ♔h2   **♔h7**

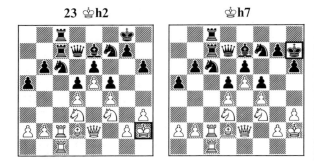

24 ♗e3   **a4**

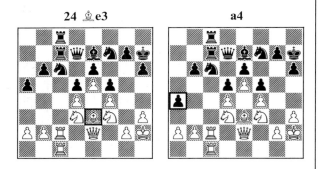

While Short has maintained his policy of masterly inaction, Kasparov has succeeded in creating some activity on the a-file. Black's threat is now ...♘a5, so Short hastens to prevent this.

25 ♗d2   **a3**

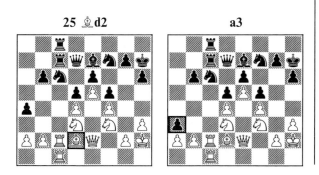

26 b3

26 b×a3 ♗×a3 27 ♖b1 allows the typically Kasparovian tactical riposte 27 ... ♘×d4!! 28 ♘×d4 (28 ♖×c7 ♘×f3+) 28 ... ♖×c2 29 ♘×c2 ♖×c2 when Black wins a pawn and also establishes a highly unpleasant pin along White's second rank.

26 ... ♘a7

Grand manœuvres commence once again, but now, at long last, Kasparov has something to bite on. The far-flung black pawn at a3 represents a real menace to the white camp. Evidently, the white pawn at a2 currently blocks the path of this pawn to coronation, but it is not inconceivable that sacrificial combinations at a later stage of the game might wipe out White's pawns on a2 and b3. In that case the black a3 pawn would represent a terrible weapon in the World Champion's hands.

27 ♗e1

Short is not averse to a mass exchange along the c-file.

27 ... ⟨Rook⟩×c2

31 ⟨Queen⟩×b5

28 ⟨Rook⟩×c2   **⟨Knight⟩d8**

White must acquiesce in the exchange of queens, otherwise Black's queen would occupy too powerful and potentially intrusive a station on b5.

31 ... ⟨Knight⟩×b5

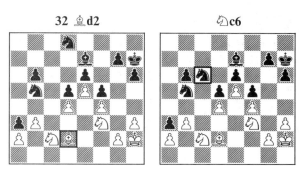

29 ⟨Knight⟩b4   **⟨Rook⟩×c2**

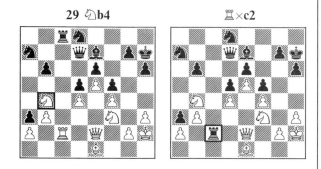

32 ⟨Bishop⟩d2   **⟨Knight⟩c6**

30 ⟨Knight⟩×c2   **⟨Queen⟩b5!**

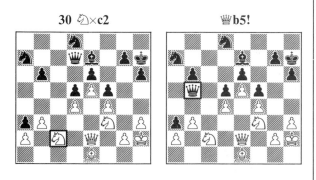

33 ⟨King⟩g1

The time has come to trade queens. With only minor pieces (bishops and knights) left on the board, Black's chances of exploiting his minute advantage are somewhat increased.

White rushes his king over to the centre and queen's wing where Black's main offensive seems in motion.

33 ... ♔g6

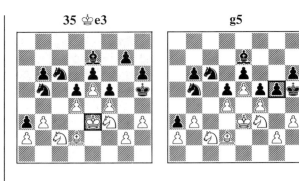

Black does the same, or is this a cunning feint? In fact, Kasparov now has a threat which Short absolutely overlooks.

The key advance has been achieved and White now finds himself in distinct difficulties.

34 ♔f2?

Probably the losing move, incredible as it may seem in such a simplified situation. White has to play 34 g4! in order to bar the advance of the black king to h5. After the likely sequence 34 ... f×g4 35 h×g4 h5 36 g×h5+ ♔×h5 37 ♔f2, as indicated by Kasparov in post-mortem analysis, Black cannot play 37 ... ♔g4 on account of 38 ♘e3+ ♔×f4 39 ♘×d5 discovered check. After 34 g4! Short should have been able to draw. Now, on the contrary, Kasparov whips up a tremendous initiative.

34 ... ♔h5!

Short had only been expecting 34 ... ♔f7. Black's plan of ... g5, gaining space and threatening to drive away White's knight with ... g4, cannot be circumvented.

35 ♔e3   g5

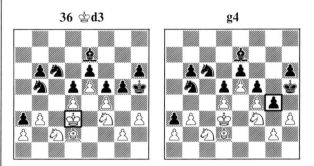

36 ♔d3   g4

Forcing the retreat of White's hitherto well-placed defensive knight.

37 ♘g1?

This particular retreat is felled by a spectacular Kasparov sacrifice which is even more surprising given the paucity of material on the board. However, after 37 ♘e1 Black wins easily with 37 ... g×h3 38 g×h3 ♔h4. If instead 37 h×g4 Black has the pleasant choice between 37 ... f×g4 and 37 ... ♔×g4 38 ♘e3+ ♔g3 (not ... ♔×f4?) and if 39 ♗e1+ then ... ♔×f4 40 ♗d2 ♘b4+ is quite safe for Black.

37 ... ♞c×d4!!

A massive blow to the very foundations of the white position. This obviously came as a terrible shock to Short.

38 h×g4+?

This should wait. The exchange of pawns merely invites Black's king to nest amongst White's weakened kingside pawns.

38 ... ♚×g4

39 ♞×d4   **♞×d4**

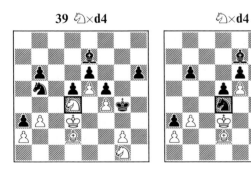

40 ♗e3

If 40 ♚×d4 ♗c5+ wins back the knight on g1. With the text Short pins his hopes on attacking Black's knight with the bishop, thus winning the pawn on b6.

40 ... ♞×b3!!

Another hammer-blow, after which White's position collapses in rubble. This is the combination, or a variation of it, which Kasparov had in mind 15 moves earlier when he advanced his a-pawn to a3. If now 41 a×b3 a2 42 ♗d4 ♗c5! and White has no good moves left.

White's coming resistance, bedevilled by frantic shortage of time, is quite futile.

41 ♗×b6   **♞c1+**

42 ♚c2   **♞×a2**

Black's position is completely winning. He is two pawns ahead, he has a monstrous passed pawn on a3 and what is left of White's ramshackle kingside pawn army is at the mercy of the black king.

43 ♘e2

♘b4+

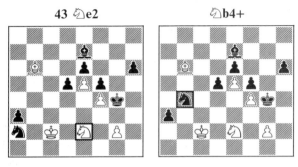

44 ♔b3

a2

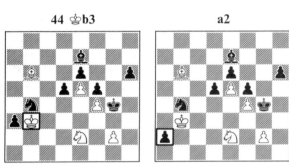

45 ♗d4

h5

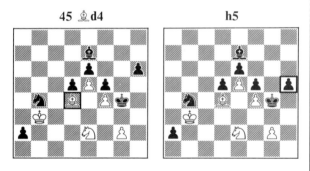

Black cannot hang on to his passed a-pawn, but he will win comfortably by transferring his pieces towards the other wing, decimating White's pawns there and then advancing his own h-pawn.

46 ♗c3

♘d3

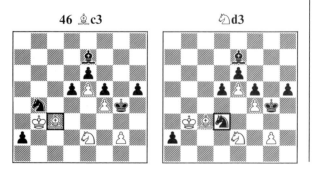

47 g3

♔f3

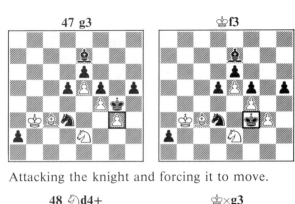

Attacking the knight and forcing it to move.

48 ♘d4+

♔×g3

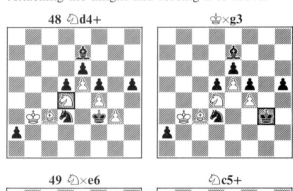

49 ♘×e6

♘c5+

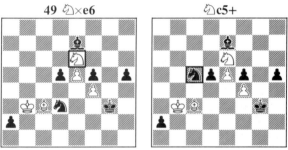

50 ♘×c5

♗×c5

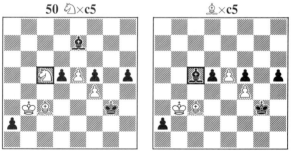

51 ♔×a2

h4

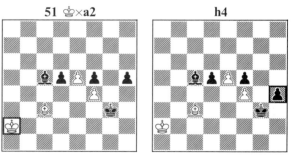

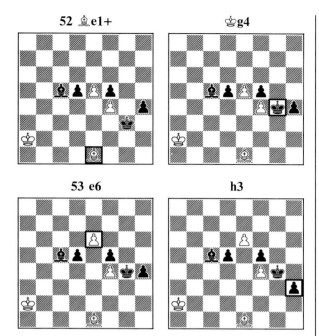

52 ♗e1+   **♔g4**

53 e6   **h3**

White has a passed pawn of his own, but it is no match for Black's storming down the h-file.

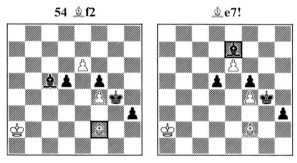

54 ♗f2   **♗e7!**

The most accurate. There is no necessity to play 54 . . . ♗×f2 55 e7 h2 56 e8=♕.

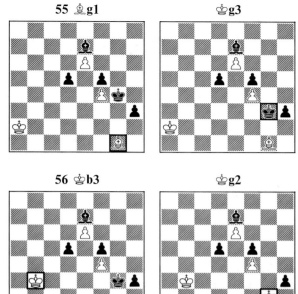

55 ♗g1   **♔g3**

56 ♔b3   **♔g2**

White resigns

After 57 ♗d4 h2 Black will promote to a queen next move.

A strategic masterpiece by the World Champion.

SCORE SO FAR:

	1	2	3	4	5	6
Kasparov	1	1	0	1		
Short	0	0	1	0		

GAME FIVE

White: Gary Kasparov   Black: Nigel Short

Old Indian Defence

A tragedy for Nigel, who had to win in order to stave off overall match defeat. The British Grandmaster selected a highly unusual defence which led to a cramped position. But Kasparov chose too direct a method of frontal attack with his knights. Gradually the Champion was driven back by Short's subtle defensive manœuvres.

Having recovered from his dubious opening, Nigel worked up a tremendous counteroffensive. His rooks seized control of a key central file, while his knight and kingside pawns combined to launch a fierce onslaught against the Champion's king, stripping away the defensive wall protecting it.

At the moment of extreme crisis, however, Nigel's nerves cracked. First he missed an opportunity to win, then he threw away the chance to draw and salvage half a point. As the game drew to its close intense awareness of the drama unfolding before them gripped the audience. Both players' clock flags were poised to fall, but Nigel, with only knight for rook, stood much worse.

The two Grandmasters on the stage fired off move after move. The clock buttons crashed like sledgehammers, but during the rush Nigel's flag fell. He had lost the game by time-forfeit, the only case of this in the match.

Both clocks have an independent mechanism and only one clock can run at any time. The minute hand picks up a 'flag' as it moves up to the vertical and this falls exactly on the hour, indicating that the player's time has expired.

2 d4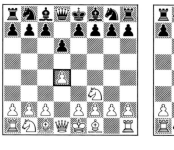

♗ g4

Once again Short chooses an unorthodox defence as Black. The assumption must be that he wanted to throw Kasparov on his own resources and eliminate the World Champion's meticulous theoretical preparation.

3 e4

Not unnaturally, White seizes the opportunity to take over the centre with his pawns.

1 ♘f3

d6

3 . . . ♘f6

4 ♘c3

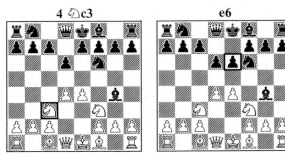

e6

A superior and more solid alternative to 4 . . . g6 (planning to develop the black king's bishop at g7) which, however, is also playable.

5 ♗e2

♗e7

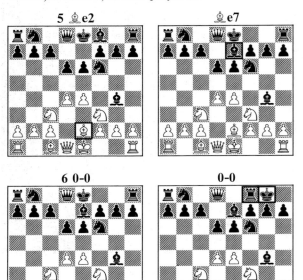

6 0-0

0-0

Perhaps Short's opening was inspired by that of the game Andersson-Korchnoi from the Wijk aan Zee tournament where Nigel had recently shared first prize. On that occasion, the same position had been reached as after Black's sixth move here, but White proceeded with 7 h3 ♗h5 8 ♗e3 ♘bd7 9 ♘d2 ♗×e2 10 ♘×e2 c5 11 c3 ♕c7 12 ♘g3 when Black experienced no difficulty in establishing an equal position.

7 ♗e3

♘bd7

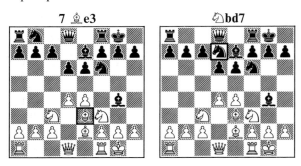

8 ♘d2

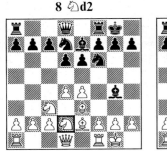

♗×e2

9 ♕×e2

This way of recapturing is more aggressive than Andersson's decision to take on e2 with the knight.

9 . . . c5

Also worth consideration are: 9 . . . c6 and 9 . . . d5.

10 d×c5

Kasparov steers for a small, but distinct, advantage, quite appropriate when leading in a six-game match by the score of 3-1. On another occasion the World Champion might have tried the more risky, but more ambitious, 10 d5.

"This match is slipping away from me and I think he knows it!"

10 . . . ♘×c5

11 ♗×c5

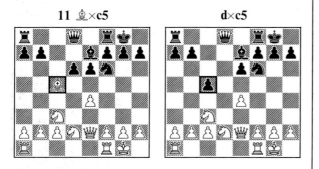

d×c5

12 ♘c4

♕c7

13 a4

This secures the position of White's aesthetically-placed knight on c4. Furthermore, the advance of White's a-pawn fixes Black's queenside pawns as a potential target for the endgame.

13 . . . ♖ad8

14 e5?!

This bold thrust looks tremendously strong since Black's knight is attacked and White appears to secure an advanced post on d6 as an attacking base for his knights. Nevertheless, by wonderfully subtle play, Short succeeds in demonstrating that this concept is erroneous. As a stronger plan the simple ♖ad1 comes into consideration.

14 . . . ♘d5

15 ♘e4

♘b6

16 ♘cd6?

This is definitely wrong. White can still maintain a slight edge by means of 16 ♘×b6 ♛×b6 17 c3.

16 . . . f5!

A marvellous move which underlines the flaw in White's calculations. White cannot play 17 e×f6 *ep* since . . . ♗×d6 wins a piece. White is, therefore, forced to retreat.

17 ♘c3   **a6!**

Not 17 . . . ♗×d6 18 ♘d5. Short's move deprives White's knight of access to b5.

18 a5   **♘d5**

19 ♘c4

The upshot of White's mistaken manœuvre has been a significant loss of time with his knights. This enables Short to strike out with a major counterattack on the kingside and in the centre.

19 . . . ♘f4

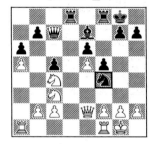

20 ♛f3   **♜d4!**

A dual-purpose move. Black defends his knight while simultaneously attacking White's on c4.

21 b3   **♘g6**

A very strong alternative is 21 . . . g5 planning to harry the white queen by . . . g4.

22 ℤfe1   **ℤf4**

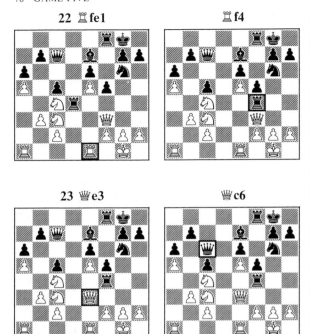

23 ♛e3   **♛c6**

Black introduces his queen into the attack against the white king. Sinister threats such as . . . ℤg4 or . . . ♞h4 are now looming, so Kasparov hastens to block the black queen's diagonal towards g2.

24 f3   **♝g5**

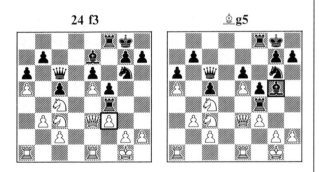

Obviously played with evil intentions against the white queen. In view of this, the World Champion is obliged to cede even more ground.

25 ♛e2   **ℤd4**

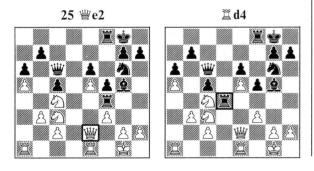

Black's rook returns to dominate the d-file and the further threat of . . . ♞f4 entices White to loosen the pawn carapace around his king.

26 g3   **ℤf8-d8**

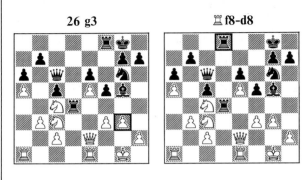

27 ℤa1-d1   **♝e7**

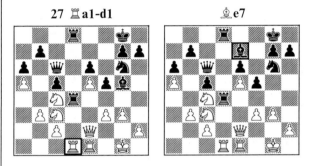

28 ♛g2

White hopes to play f4, challenging the black queen. Short promptly stamps on this possibility of freedom for his opponent.

28 . . . f4!

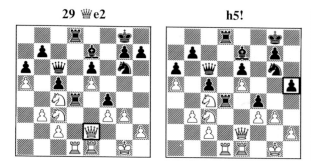

29 ♕e2   **h5!**

Wonderfully aggressive play by Nigel, who seeks to strip away the pawn protection surrounding the white king even if it means exposing his own king to possible counter-punches.

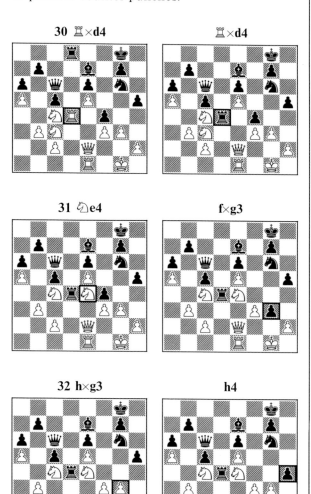

30 ♖×d4   **♖×d4**

31 ♘e4   **f×g3**

32 h×g3   **h4**

Absolutely consistent with his previous policy. Black's intention is to gain control of the f4 square for his knight. At this moment, both players had

around seven minutes to complete all their moves. This must have been torment in such a complex situation.

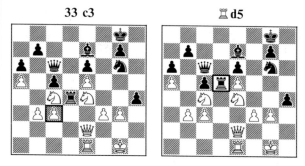

33 c3   **♖d5**

Attacking White's pawn on e5. White's next few moves are forced.

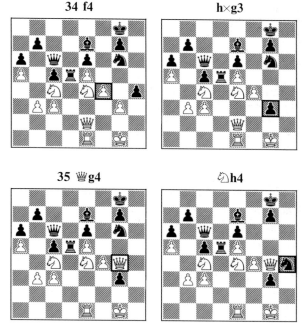

34 f4   **h×g3**

35 ♕g4   **♘h4**

Again the most ambitious move from Nigel.

36 ♘f6+

White's only counter-chance.

36 . . . ♗×f6

37 e×f6

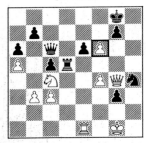

The absolute crisis of the game. Black is a pawn ahead, but he is threatened with mate by ♕×g7. Furthermore, Black's knight on h4 is under attack. To compound matters White threatens a terrible invasion at e5 with his knight.

This is a position which calls for the utmost resolution, but it is at this moment, with his clock time draining away, that Nigel falters. The only correct move, and one which Kasparov demonstrated to his stunned opponent at the conclusion of the game, is 37 . . . g5!! There are now some fascinating variations:

  1) 38 ♖×e6? ♖d1+! 39 ♕×d1 ♕g2 checkmate.
  2) 38 ♕×e6+ ♕×e6 39 ♖×e6 ♖d1+ wins for Black.
  3) 38 ♘e5? ♖×e5! followed by . . . ♕g2 mate.
  4) 38 f×g5 ♖d2! with terrible threats.
  5) 38 ♘e3 (the best chance) 38 . . . ♖e5!! 39 f×e5 ♘f3+ 40 ♔g2 ♘×e5 discovered check 41 ♔×g3 ♘×g4 42 ♘×g4 ♕c7+ and Black has excellent chances to win.

Fantastic possibilities!

37 . . . ♘f5?

Missing his chance to win.

38 ♘e5

Nigel now hesitated, agonisingly, until almost all of his remaining time had vanished. At last he moved . . . .

38 . . . ♕d6

39 ♕h5   **♖×e5!**

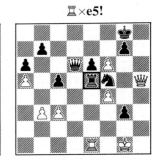

Black had to destroy this horrible beast even at the price of his rook.

40 ♖×e5   **♕d2!**

Even now, Black should not lose, since White's king is horrifically exposed to a cascade of checks from the black queen. But Nigel had almost no time in which to make his moves.

"I wish I had more time to think about this move!"

41 ♕e2

♕×c3

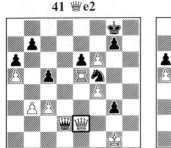

42 ♖×e6

43 ♔g2

g×f6

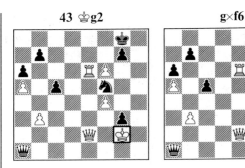
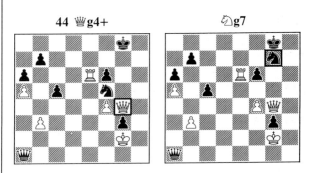

Played reluctantly by a demoralised Short who by now had realised that his attacking chances had evaporated completely.

The Champion is about to launch his own attack. If a saving grace exists, it must be now, but Nigel's flag is hanging, poised to fall and condemn him to loss of the game by time forfeit. There is indeed a save, but can Nigel find it before the axe descends?

44 ♕g4+

♘g7

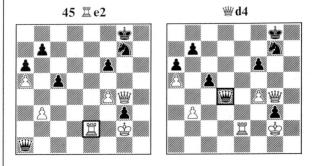

42 ... ♕a1+??

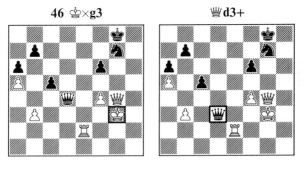

45 ♖e2

♕d4

46 ♔×g3

♕d3+

The losing blunder. Nigel had to play 42 ... ♕d4+ 43 ♔g2 (43 ♔f1? ♕×f4+) 43 ... ♕d5+ 44 ♕e4 (not 44 ♔h3 ♕h1+ 45 ♔g4 g2) 44 ... ♕d2+ and White must take a draw with 45 ♕e2 ♕d5+ rather than run the gauntlet of 45 ♔h3 ♕h2+ 46 ♔g4 ♕h4+ 47 ♔f3 (47 ♔×f5?? ♕h5 mate) 47 ... ♕h5+ 48 ♔g2 ♕h2+. In all of these lines Black has at least a draw. Short's move in the game removes his queen from contact with the white king and thus annihilates Black's chances of reaching a draw through perpetual check.

White has a rook for a knight in an open position. On top of this, Kasparov now has the initiative.

47 ♔g2   **♛×b3**

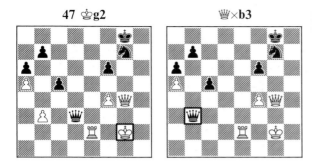

48 ♕f3   **♕f7**

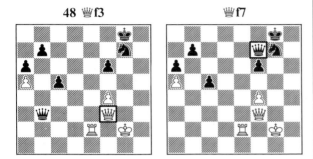

Both players were making their moves instantaneously.

49 ♕e4   **c4**

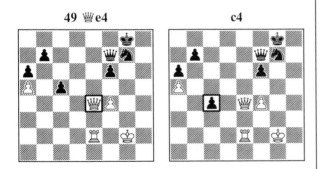

50 ♖c2

Black's c-pawn is doomed.

50 . . . ♔f8

51 ♖×c4   **♘e8**

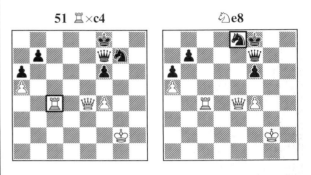

52 ♖c8

At this point the players were banging down their moves at such a furious rate that even our special computer (programmed to cope with no less than nine consecutive moves at half-second intervals) could not follow the play.

A couple more 'unimportant moves' (according to Kasparov) were played and then . . . .

Black lost on time

Although his position is a technical loss, there is still some fight left and no-one would dream of conceding the game at this stage were it not for the time forfeit.

THE SCORE SO FAR:

	1	2	3	4	5	6
Kasparov	1	1	0	1	1	
Short	0	0	1	0	0	

GAME SIX

White: Nigel Short   Black: Gary Kasparov
Sicilian Defence

Nigel strikes back to take the sixth game. During the course of the 20th century only six British wins have been registered against reigning World Champions. And of those six, Nigel Short, just 21 years old, has now scored no less than three!

Short was rocked back on his heels in the opening. Kasparov's habitual Sicilian counter-attack came with incredible speed and Short was caught with his defences down. White's pieces were chased back in confusion and weaknesses sprang up in his position.

However, in the middlegame Kasparov repeatedly hesitated. He undertook unnecessary defensive manœuvres, mishandled his attack against the white king and permitted Short's pieces to seize vital central posts. In fact, when Gary launched his final desperate attack, bombarding the white fortifications with violent sacrifices, he had already been thoroughly outmanœuvred by the young British genius.

With this win Nigel had clinched the final victory of this historic match and exceeded the expectations of pre-match expert prediction.

Chess connoisseurs present had become convinced that the young Englishman can really challenge for the world title in the not too distant future.

Both players deserve tremendous credit for their fighting spirit and will to win. Every single game produced entertainment of the highest quality, and there was not one drawn game!

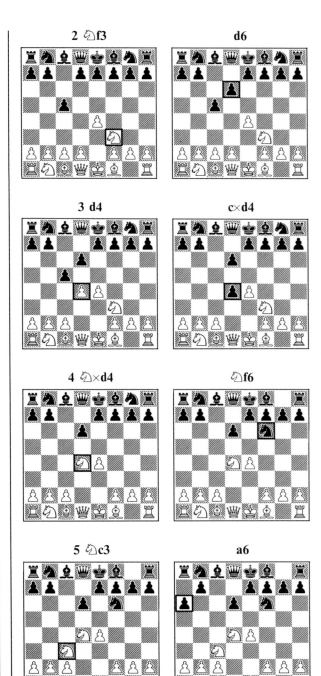

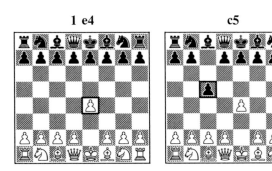

6 ♗e3

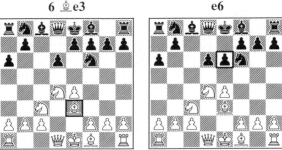

e6

7 f3

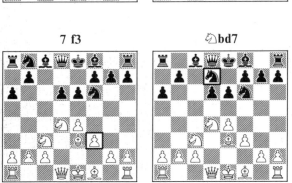

♘bd7

8 g4

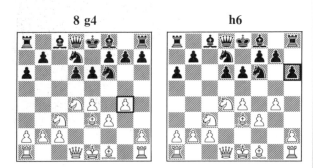

h6

9 h4

Up to this point the game is an exact duplication of the Sicilian Najdorf variation which had been played in Game Two of this match. On that earlier occasion, Kasparov had continued with 9 . . . b5. In the interim, the World Champion had subjected this opening to careful scrutiny. Now he comes up with a major improvement.

9 . . . ♘e5!

10 ♖g1?

Surprised by the innovation, Nigel goes astray. The correct course is 10 ♕e2, planning 0-0-0. After White's error Kasparov immediately captures the initiative.

10 . . . ♕b6!

The threat to take White's pawn on b2 is so often illusory, but in this case it is absolutely real. White must protect b2. Short's choice appears terribly passive, but 11 ♖b1 (the main alternative) would deprive White of the possibility of castling queen-side and in this resides White's only hope of tangible counterplay.

11 ♕c1

d5!

"What has gone wrong with my beautiful position?"

The World Champion continues to handle the opening with wonderful energy. An interesting, if absolutely unnecessary, alternative is 11 ... ♛×d4 12 ♗×d4 ♘×f3+ 13 ♔f2 ♘×d4. Black would have two minor pieces and a pawn for the queen, but it would hardly be sound.

12 ♗e2   d×e4

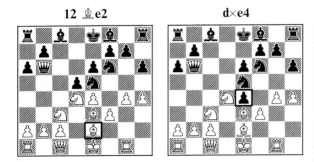

If 12 ... ♗c5 13 ♛d2 ♛×b2 14 ♖b1 ♛a3 15 g5 and White succeeds in confusing the issue. Kasparov's method establishes a clear strategic advantage for Black.

13 ♘×e4   ♘×e4

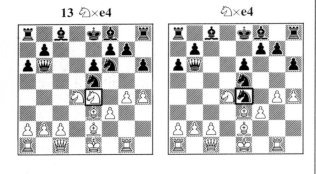

14 f×e4   ♗e7

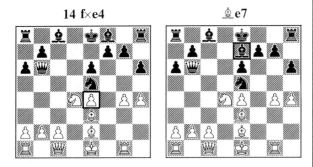

The threat to capture on h4 with check forces White into a humiliating retraction of his tenth move.

15 ♖h1   ♗d7

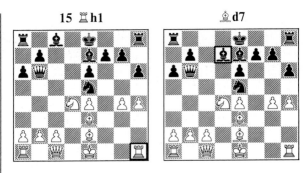

It looks as if White will ultimately have the choice of castling either on the kingside or on the queenside. However, the fact that White has already moved his king's rook rules out the former option.

16 c3   ♛c7

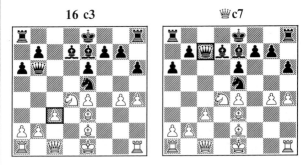

With the cunning threat of ... ♘×g4 followed by ... ♛g3+. Nigel takes measures to prevent this devious trick.

17 ♗f2   b5

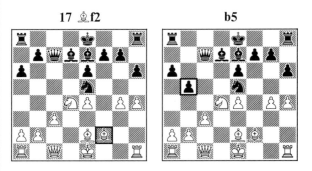

Taking stock of the position it is evident that Black has the advantage. White has three groups of rather shaky pawns and Black's knight on e5 radiates strength. White's only chance in the future course of the game is to hurl his two kingside pawns forwards in order to come to grips with the black king.

18 ♕c2

♘c4

An interesting decision. Most players would have maintained the black knight on its excellent post with . . . b4 or perhaps . . . ♖c8. Kasparov, however, has identified White's king's bishop as a key defensive piece and wishes to force its exchange.

20 . . . ♕c7

21 0-0-0

White does not fear 21 . . . ♕f4+ 22 ♔b2 ♕×g4 23 ♖hg1 with a counterattack on the g-file. Having castled queenside White has succeeded in restoring a semblance of order to his position.

19 ♗×c4

♕×c4

One can gauge the impact of Gary's novel opening by the fact that Nigel had only 11½ minutes left at this juncture while Black had 3 minutes more in hand. It is possible, though, that Black's 19th move is incorrect. It might have been profitably replaced with 19 . . . b×c4 intending to pile up against White's position by later doubling rooks on the open b-file.

21 . . . 0-0

20 b3

White is obliged to weaken his c3 pawn in this fashion if he wishes to castle his king into safety. 20 0-0-0 is forbidden on account of . . . ♕×a2.

22 ♔b1

a5

Here comes Black's attack against the white king. White must react quickly on the other wing.

23 g5   **h5!**

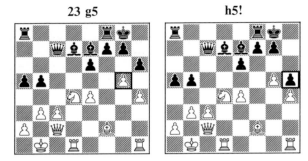

Naturally, Black does not hand White attacking chances almost free of charge with the greedy 23 . . .h×g5 24 h×g5 ♗×g5 25 e5, when White threatens mate on h7.

24 ♖hg1   **a4?**

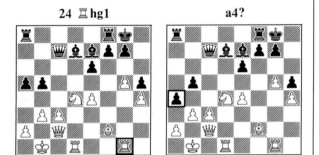

The wrong way of prosecuting his assault. This move permits White to block off most avenues of attack on the queen's wing. A more promising course would have been the pawn sacrifice 24 . . . b4!? 25 c×b4 ♕b7. Alternatively, 24 . . . b4 and if White tries to set up a barricade with 25 c4 then . . . a4 is now appropriate, prising open the a-file for a future attack.

25 b4!

Suddenly it is not so easy. Nigel's position has become more co-ordinated and there is no clear way for Black to proceed.

25 . . . ♖ac8

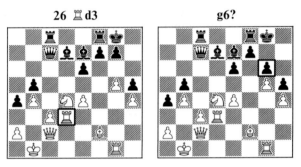

26 ♖d3   **g6?**

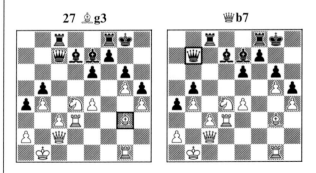

There was no necessity for this defensive move which creates significant weaknesses in the e5-h8 diagonal. Short is not slow to exploit this.

27 ♗g3   **♕b7**

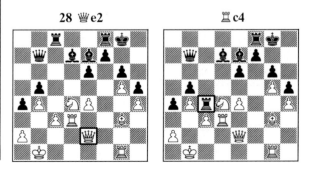

28 ♕e2   **♖c4**

29 ♗e5!

White's bishop now occupies a splendid diagonal. From e5 this piece not only scythes into the black kingside, but also defends backwards against Kasparov's threatened offensive directed towards the white king.

29 . . . ♖fc8

30 ♕e3   ♗c6

31 ♖e1   a3

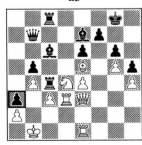

When he played this, Kasparov undoubtedly

believed that he was closing the net around the white king. The situation is reminiscent of the play in Game Four, where Kasparov won by means of a pawn stuck in White's gullet on a3. The difference is that White has manœuvred with wonderful subtlety to gain distinct counterchances of his own against the black king.

32 ♕f4!

It might appear that Kasparov now has a devastating sacrificial combination at his fingertips, namely 32 . . . ♗×b4 33 c×b4 ♗×e4 34 ♖×e4 ♕×e4 35 ♕×e4 ♖c1 checkmate. However, the interpolation 33 ♕f6! foils all of this ingenuity and leaves Black facing checkmate.

32 . . . ♗e8

33 ♘b3

White now has two deadly threats: ♘a5 and ♗d4 followed by ♕e5. Gary decides to set a trap to deal with the first threat, but as it turns out, the trapper is trapped.

33 . . . ♛c6

The spectators were riveted. Will he or won't he play ♘a5 ? At first sight this seems to win the exchange (Black's rook for White's knight). On closer examination, Black has a devastating counter.

34 ♘a5

Brilliancy or blunder?

34 . . . ♜×b4+

White appears to be crushed, since 35 c×b4 permits the devastating . . . ♛c2+. But Nigel has seen further than everyone, including the World Champion.

35 ♔a1!!

This cool retreat into the corner leaves Black with his queen and rook under attack. Kasparov now tries some highly ingenious last-minute sacrifices, but they are doomed to failure against Short's icily accurate defence.

35 . . . ♛c5

36 c×b4 ♛×b4

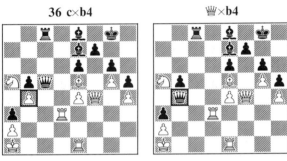

Threatening . . . ♛×a5 and ♛×e1+. There is only one move.

37 ♛d2! ♜c2

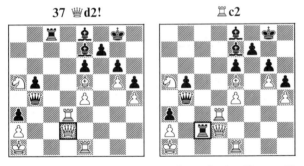

A spectacular detonation of tactical effects. 38 ♛×c2 ♛×e1+ followed by . . . ♛×a5 still permits Black to resist. Short's path is more accurate.

38 ♛×b4 ♗×b4

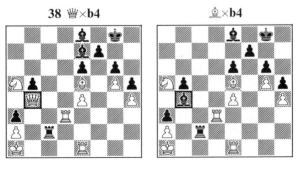

39 ♖d8   **f6**

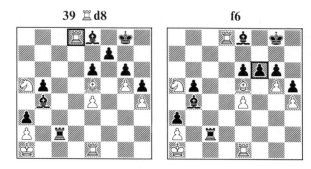

Necessary to prevent checkmate. Some confusion
still persists since White, though a rook ahead, and
attacking Black's queen's bishop with check, still
has three pieces of his own under fire.

40 ♖f1   **f×e5**

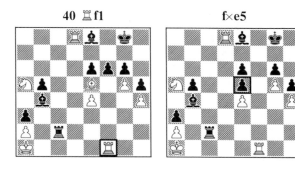

41 ♖×e8+   **♔g7**

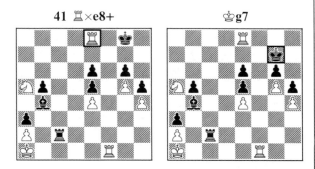

42 ♘b3   **♗c3+**

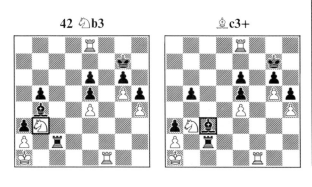

43 ♔b1   **♖b2+**

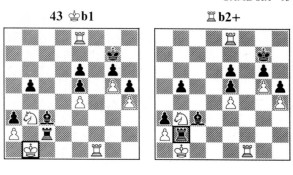

44 ♔c1

Black's position must be hopeless, but he could
avoid immediate resignation by playing 44 . . .
♖×a2. In trying for a final combination Kasparov
overlooks a short circuit.

44 . . . ♖×b3?

45 ♔c2!

Forking Black's last remaining pieces.

Black resigned

An extraordinary comeback by Nigel Short, who
seemed amazingly fresh at the end in spite of the
physical and mental exertions demanded by this
tense and gruelling match.

George Walden MP, Under-Secretary of State for Higher Education, presents the London Docklands Trophy to the victorious Gary Kasparov.

Prize-giving Ceremony

The handsome winner's trophy, a crafted, engraved bowl offered by the London Docklands Development Corporation, was presented to Gary Kasparov by George Walden MP, Under-Secretary of State for Higher Education. Sharing the platform of honour was Jennifer Dabo, representing the LDDC.

The minister drew attention to England's outstanding record in chess, second only to that of Gary's homeland, the USSR, and prophesied an even more successful future. It was entirely appropriate that the Education Minister should have officiated at this ceremony, since the important rôle chess plays in education has been firmly established.

After the ceremony, players, officials, journalists and invited guests transferred to nearby Stringfellows nightclub to enjoy hospitality courtesy of flamboyant owner and entrepreneur, Peter Stringfellow, himself.

At the close a tired, but victorious Kasparov stated that Nigel Short had made tremendous progress in recent months and in a year would be clearly established as the major western contender for the World Title.

The players, officials and invited guests. <u>Left to Right</u>: Bob Wade, OBE, IM (arbiter); Nigel Short GM; Jennifer Dabo (LDDC); George Walden, MP; Gary Kasparov, World Champion; Louise McDonald (arbiter); Lothar Schmid, GM (arbiter).

Match Result

London Hippodrome, Leicester Square, 4 and 5 February 1987

	1	2	3	4	5	6	Total
Gary Kasparov	1	1	0	1	1	0	**4 points**
Nigel Short	0	0	1	0	0	1	**2 points**

Still smiling after two days' hard work, Gary Kasparov chats with Channel 4 presenter, Tony Bastable.